The Holy Spirit

The Holy Spirit

Font of Love, Life, and Power

* * * * *

MARY KATHLEEN GLAVICH, SND

Contents

Introduction

At first I was tempted to title this book "The Holy Spirit: Our Superhero." Since the 1930s, people have been intrigued with superheroes like Superman, Batman, Wonder Woman, Captain America, and Spider-Man. According to Wikipedia, a superhero is someone "usually possessing supernatural or superhuman powers, who is dedicated to fighting the evil of their universe, protecting the public, and usually battling supervillains." When you think about it, that is a fitting description for the Holy Spirit! Let me explain.

This Person of the Trinity possesses incredible superhuman powers because he* is God, the Supreme Being. As the absolute good, the Holy Spirit works to vanquish all forms of evil. His archenemy is the ultimate villain, Satan, who is compared to a roaring lion prowling around "looking for someone to devour" (1 Peter 5:8). The Holy Spirit is constantly present with us and within us, protecting, guiding, enlightening, and strengthening.

At every Sunday Mass as we pray the Nicene Creed, we acknowledge the Holy Spirit as "the Lord, the giver of life."

---

* In this book for the sake of convenience masculine pronouns are used to refer to the Holy Spirit, who, being a pure spirit, actually has no gender.

7

Not only is he the source of our life, but he is devoted to ensuring that our lives are safe and happy here on Earth and continue happily in the kingdom of heaven.

In view of who the Holy Spirit is as well as his intimate connection to our lives and well-being, you would conclude that he is foremost in our minds and prayers. Ironically and sadly, most people pay scant attention to him so that the Spirit has been called "the Cinderella" of the Trinity. For many years, I too was one of those unenlightened people.

Then one day my spiritual director asked, "Do you ever pray to the Holy Spirit?" "Not really," I answered. "You, a writer?" he asked, his eyebrows raised.

From then on, I cultivated a friendship with this mysterious Spirit, and he has come to my defense and empowered me on numerous occasions. For example, the Holy Spirit rightly could be called the co-author of my books. (A witty friend suggested that the Spirit is my ghostwriter!)

The catalyst for my writing a book about the Holy Spirit occurred as I was selling my books at my parish. Dominic, a successful businessman, approached me and said, "Would you write a book on the Holy Spirit? I don't understand him." I promised Dominic that I would—and I like to keep my promises.

The Holy Spirit: Font of Love, Life, and Power is geared to the average man or woman. It presents some of the great truths about our triune God, in particular the Spirit, in plain English. Each chapter opens with a quotation linked to its topic and concludes with questions for reflection or discussion, a prayer—to the Holy Spirit, of course—and an action. The Appendix contains a collection of prayers to him gleaned from various sources.

Although the Holy Spirit is a mysterious, invisible Person, symbols have arisen that provide glimpses into who he is and what he does. Among them are wind, breath, fire, water, cloud, dove, seal, and dew. These metaphors associated with the Spirit appear in the Old and New Testaments, and most of them are explained in gray boxes in the following pages.

I hope that through this book people will become more aware of their invisible Friend and lifelong Companion and establish a relationship with him as I did. Then they too will be inclined to pray, "Come, Holy Spirit," and experience the power of this precious Gift whom Jesus and the Father sent us. They will learn to "walk in the Spirit."

1

God the Holy Spirit

O eternal Trinity, You are a deep sea
in which the more I seek, the more I find,
and the more I find, the more I seek to know You.
~ St. Catherine of Siena

One evening during a thunderstorm a frightened little girl scampered from her bed to her mother. Holding the child on her lap, the mother soothed, "Don't be afraid. God is always with you." "I know that," the girl replied, "but I want someone with skin."

God is pure spirit. Not only is he skinless, but immaterial. He has no parts and doesn't occupy space. You can't see, hear, or feel God, just as you can't perceive your soul (your spiritual component) with your senses.

As a Christian, you believe in the Trinity, one God in three distinct Persons: the Father, the First Person; the Son, the Second Person; and the Holy Spirit, the Third Person. A person has an intellect and a will and so can think, love, and choose. "Person" tells who while "nature" tells what. The Trinity is three Persons in one nature—a divine nature.

Whenever you make the Sign of the Cross over your body, think: God, I offer you my whole self.

First-century Christians believed the Spirit was God. When Ananias and his wife Sapphira cheated the Church, Peter accused them of lying to the Holy Spirit and then said, "You did not lie to us but to God!" (Acts 5:4).

You acknowledge all three Persons in some familiar prayers. Praying the Sign of the Cross, you make a cross over yourself while saying, "In the name of the Father, and of the Son, and of the Holy Spirit." Blessings are usually imparted using these same words, for example, when a priest blesses you at Mass and when you bless yourself with holy water. As you pray the Nicene Creed at Mass, you affirm the Spirit's divinity, declaring that the Holy Spirit together with the Father and the Son "is adored and glorified." Yet you might tend to neglect this Third Person.

Not being able to visualize the faceless Holy Spirit is an impediment to praying to him. We picture the Father as a bearded older man. And because the Son became a first-century Jewish man and appears in a great deal of artwork, we easily imagine him. But the Spirit remains a nebulous haze. Artists represent him as a dove because in Gospel accounts of Jesus' baptism the Holy Spirit descended on him in this form. But speaking to a dove is not exactly appealing.

Eucharistic Prayer IV of the Mass succinctly states the Spirit's job description—which is focused on us: So we might live for Jesus, he gave us the Holy Spirit "to complete his work and bring us the fullness of grace." How ironic that One who is so intimately involved in our salvation and eternal happiness is to a great extent forgotten or ignored!

One of the Godhead

The divine Persons are consubstantial. Father, Son, and Holy Spirit are all God, the Supreme Being. They are all uncreated; no one made God. In addition, the Persons are eternal: They have always existed and will live forever. In other words, God had no beginning and will have no end, a concept that we timebound creatures cannot wrap our minds around.

The some-what intimi-dating word *consubstantial* simply means having the same sub-stance, nature, or essence.

The three Persons are coequal. They have the same powers and qualities, and they possess them in equal degrees. No Person is greater than the others, and no one is subordinate. The Holy Spirit fully has all the divine attributes.

The Spirit is omnipotent (almighty).

" 'I am the Alpha and the Omega,' " says the Lord God, "who is and who was and who is to come, the Almighty" (Revelation 1:8).

You can trust that the Spirit has the power to accomplish great things for you and your loved ones—even things you may consider impos-sible. So be quick to ask for his help.

The Spirit is omniscient (knows all things).

"You know when I sit down and when I rise up; you discern my thoughts from far away.... Such knowledge is too wonderful for me" (Psalm 139:2, 6).

In the icon "The Trinity" by Andrei Rublev, three angels seated around a table are thought to represent the three divine Persons. The Holy Spirit's robes are blue for divinity and green for new life.

Take comfort in the fact that the Holy Spirit is aware of every moment of your life and every aspect, including the secrets of your heart. He knows your entire life: your past, present, and future. He knows why you do things and your deepest desires. In fact, he knows you better than anyone—including yourself!

The Spirit is omnipresent (everywhere).

"Where can I go from your spirit? / Or where can I flee from your presence? If I ascend to heaven, you are there; / if I make my bed in Sheol, you are there" (Psalm 139:7–8).

No matter where you are—lost in a foreign country, flying 35,000 miles above the Earth, or walking down a dark, deserted street—the Spirit is your companion. You need not fear.

The Spirit has other infinite perfections.

"The LORD is gracious and merciful, slow to anger and abounding in steadfast love" (Psalm 145:8).

Like God the Father and God the Son, God the Holy Spirit is perfect in every way. He possesses absolutely all the qualities that you admire. He is all-holy, all-good, all-just, all-merciful, all-faithful, all-beautiful, and all-loving. Surely the Spirit is the best kind of friend you could ever have.

The Spirit is immutable (unchanging).

"I the LORD do not change" (Malachi 3:6).

You pray, "As it was in the beginning, is now, and ever shall be." The Spirit is always perfect. He is not moody or fickle. You can count on him to always be the same. His love and concern for you is constant—no matter how imperfect you are.

Attributions

Because God is one and indivisible, the three divine Persons act together. This means that all three of them created, all redeemed, and all work to make us holy. That is why St. Irenaeus could say, "God has created the world with his two hands, the Son and the Spirit."

The divine Persons, though, are distinct. Flowing from their roles in their innermost life, we assign actions that impact us human beings to the individual Persons: creation to the Father, redemption to the Son, and sanctification to the Holy Spirit. The Third Person brings the work of the Trinity to completion.

You, who are made in the image and likeness of God and who are his adopted child, can participate in the Trinity's activities in the following ways:

Theologians refer to the Blessed Persons in roles that involve humans as the economic Trinity and the Persons in regard to their inner relationships as the immanent Trinity.

Imitating the Divine Persons' Work

• You resemble God the Father, the Creator, whenever you produce something such as a new recipe, a piece of artwork, or a poem. As creator, God brings forth life. You bring forth life by having children and also by nurturing the lives of other people: family members, friends, and even strangers. You foster life by planting gardens, caring for pets, and supporting organizations that try to prevent the extinction of endangered species. You also participate in creation when you take a stand against abortion that snuffs out life at its beginning stages and when you work to abolish the death penalty.

• You are like God the Son, the Redeemer who sacrificed his life so that we might live forever, when you donate your time, talents, and money to improving the quality of someone else's life. You might sacrifice your ego and let another person be praised for a job. You might forgo doing something that gives you pleasure (like watching a movie) in order to help someone else achieve a goal (like moving into a nursing home). You might stay up late at night to quiet a crying baby or to minister to a sick person. You might donate blood or even a kidney!

• You imitate the Holy Spirit, who enlightens us and makes us holy, when you teach someone about the faith, share a book about it, or invite someone to church or to a lecture or a course on the faith. You might give a backslider a little boost toward holiness by having the courage to point out a fault. And you can influence people to become better persons by modeling various virtues.

An Impossibility

St. Augustine (354–430), bishop of Hippo, wrote the treatise *On the Trinity*. It's said that one day as he strolled along a beach, pondering the inscrutable mystery of God, he came upon a strange scene. A boy was repeatedly filling a seashell with ocean water, running to a hole in the sand, and pouring in the water. "What are you doing?" the saint inquired. The lad replied, "I'm putting the whole sea into this hole." St. Augustine smiled and said, "But that's impossible." The child declared, "It's just as impossible for you to comprehend the Trinity with your small mind." Then the boy vanished.

The "lad" was right. We will never be able to fathom the infinite Trinity with our finite minds. The Three-in-One is a strict mystery that we must accept "on faith."

So incomprehensible is the Holy Spirit in his greatness, so infinite in his loving richness, that all His greatness and infinity eludes any image our human reason could form.

~ Johannes Tauler, O.P.

Attempting to Understand the Trinity

Although we will never comprehend the inner life of the Trinity, the Church teaches how the three Persons exist. The Father is the source of the Son, while the Holy Spirit comes from the Father and Son together. We say that the Father *generates* the Son, who is *begotten*. The Holy Spirit *proceeds* from both of them in an act known as *spiration* or "breathing forth." This

In 1054 the schism between Eastern and Western Christianity occurred. The main reason was that Western Christians held that the Spirit proceeded from the Father and the Son and added *filioque* (and the Son) to the Creed. Eastern Christians believed the Spirit came from the Father period.

whole process is ongoing and simultaneous. No divine Person came first. The holy Three are eternally coexistent.

How does this divine inner life happen? Here is the proposal: Our human thoughts can be expressed as words. When God the Father thinks of himself, his thought is so powerful that it becomes the Word, the Son, who is an exact reflection of the Father. The Father and the Son behold each other's perfection and beauty. They respond with a love so immense and profound that it becomes another Person, the Holy Spirit.

This Holy Spirit is the bond of love between the Father and the Son. St. Bernard called the Spirit their mutual kiss. A lovely image of the perpetual life of the three Persons is ecstatic dancing—circling and embracing in a movement of loving attentiveness and joy. And, amazingly, they invite you to participate in their divine dance and share their life.

Metaphors have been proposed to help us understand how three entities can be one. But all of these comparisons "limp." The most famous is St. Patrick's three-leaf clover. Other metaphors are the three forms of water (solid, liquid, and gas); the components of an egg (shell, yolk, albumin); and the dimensions of space (height, width, and depth). Following are analogies that give us an inkling of how the members of the Trinity are related:

- Water is a symbol of life. The spring is the Father, rivers are the Son, and irrigation canals are the Spirit.

- The sun is the Father, the ray is the Son, and the point where the ray touches Earth is the Spirit.

- The fruit is the Holy Spirit, picked from the branch (Son) fed by the root (Father).

  – Tertullian

- Eternity is in the Father, beauty in the image [Son], and fruition in the Gift.

  – St. Hilary

- The Father is your table, the Son is your food, and the Holy Spirit waits on you and then makes His dwelling in you.

  – St. Catherine of Siena

- The mouth of God is the Holy Spirit and God's word is his Son.

  – St. Simeon the New Theologian

Native Americans often used the term Great Spirit or Great Mystery to refer to the all-encompassing power that oversaw the universe.

In William Paul Young's novel *The Shack,* the Father is a large African American woman named Papa; the Son is a Middle Eastern, Jewish workman; and the Spirit is an ethereal Asian woman who sings and tends gardens. Papa also appears as a beautiful Hispanic woman and then as a tall man with a mustache, goatee, and silver-white ponytail.

Names for God

Names represent people. That is why the second commandment forbids us to take the name of God carelessly and without reverence. Knowing someone's name is the first step in establishing a relationship. God says to us in Scripture, "I have called you by name, you are mine" (Isaiah 43:1).

When God spoke to Moses in the burning bush, he revealed his name: "I am who am." The Hebrew letters are comparable to YHWH. This was probably pronounced "yah-weh." Out of reverence the Jews substituted Adonai (my Lord) for Yahweh. Adding the vowels from Adonai to YHWH yielded the name Jehovah.

The names Father, Son, and Spirit for the Blessed Trinity are rooted in Scripture and affirmed by tradition. Alternate names have been suggested, such as Creator, Redeemer, and Sanctifier. St. Augustine, reflecting on the inner life of the three Persons, named them the Lover, the Beloved, and Love. St. Bernard called them Unity, Truth, and Goodness. Traditionally, the Father is Power, the Son is Truth, and the Holy Spirit is Love.

Richard Rohr, O.F.M., rightly stated in his Trinity prayer: "Every name falls short of your goodness and greatness." Similarly, theologian Hans Urs von Balthasar referred to the Holy Spirit as Unknown One Beyond the Word.

Why "Holy" Spirit?

Holy is God's attribute that signifies he is transcendent and awesome. Although all three Persons are all-holy, only the Third Person is given "Holy" as part of his proper name. Perhaps this is because of the Spirit's role in the life of the Trinity. Follow this logic: To be holy is to be like God, and "God is love" (1 John 4:8, 16). The Spirit is the love that binds the Trinity together. Therefore, the Spirit is holy.

This unique adjective in the Spirit's name may also stem from his task of sanctification— helping us to become holy. St. Basil wrote, "There is no holiness without the Holy Spirit."

Eastern Christians call being filled with the joy and power of God's own life at baptism "divinization."

How "Ghost" Became "Spirit"

A bit of history: Sometime in the 1950s the name Holy Ghost for the Third Person of the Trinity was largely replaced by Holy Spirit. There were good reasons for this change. The Greek word for "spirit" and "wind" is *pneuma*. St. Jerome translated this word in his Latin Bible (the Vulgate) as *spiritus*. The Old English word for spirit was *gast,* which became our modern *ghost.* Although *ghost* and *spirit* are synonyms, nowadays the term *ghost* is more identified with the spirit of a dead person. In addition, for children ghost has frightening overtones because it conjures up Halloween images: spooky figures in white sheets.

In the Universe

God's foot is so vast that this entire earth is but a field on God's toe. . . . What then is not a sanctuary? Where then can I not kneel and pray at a shrine made holy by God's presence?

~ Saint Catherine of Siena

The Holy Spirit is the life-force that dwells in every living creature and is at the heart of the universe. He is always at work everywhere, overseeing every process and holding all things together—from atoms to galaxies—moment by moment. God pervades everything in creation. God asks, "Do I not fill heaven and earth?" (Jeremiah 23:24). In the book *Divine Milieu,* Paleontologist Pierre Teilhard de Chardin, S.J., wrote, "By means of all created things without exception, the divine assails us, penetrates us, and molds us." We can say that creation is a theophany, something that reveals God to us. The whole cosmos is a burning bush!

Given that all of creation is sacred, it can be a source of prayer and lead us to God. Being convinced of creation's holiness motivates us to treat all created things—animals, forests, water, air—with reverence and take steps to ensure that they are protected.

"The whole creation has been groaning in labor pains" (Romans 18:22). Adam's sin made it subject to decay. Through the Spirit's power and grace, creation is being renewed and moving forward to the grand finale when there will be new heavens and a new earth. At that time we will return to the Father and be caught up into God. The union with God that was originally planned for us will be realized.

The Holy Spirit as Advocate

In John's Gospel, Jesus introduced the Holy Spirit at the Last Supper when he promised to ask the Father to send another Advocate (a Person, not a force). This Spirit would be the presence of Jesus for us after he ascended to heaven. The Holy Spirit is the Spirit of Jesus.

The Greek word translated in most Bibles as "advocate" is *paraclete,* a rare term only John uses in Scripture. It combines the Greek words for "alongside" and "summon" and may refer to a person who stands beside someone in a court of law—a defense attorney. All translations of "paraclete" express support. Besides advocate, these are helper, defender, comforter, counselor, strengthener, intercessor, and consoler (someone who gives courage). A friend of mine describes the Holy Spirit as "an enigmatic 'got your back' brother."

We originated from God, and the Holy Spirit's mission is to unite us intimately with God on Earth and see that we return to him.

Jesus called the Holy Spirit "another" Advocate because he himself is also our advocate.

We are to carry out the roles of paraclete for one another.

The Holy Spirit as Seal

Believers are "marked with the seal of the promised Holy Spirit" (Ephesians 1:13). A seal is stamped on a document to show ownership or approval (like the Better Business Bureau's

23

St. Simeon the New Theologian stated that the goal and purpose of all of Christ's work of salvation for us was that believers should receive the Holy Spirit.

It is on him [Jesus] that God the Father has set his seal.

~ John 6:27

seal). The Holy Spirit makes an impression on us, claiming us for God. In addition, a seal guarantees that promises will be kept. Dwelling in our hearts, the Holy Spirit "is the pledge of our inheritance" (Ephesians 1:14) as adopted children of God. He is a "first installment" (2 Corinthians 1:22) or down payment on the marvelous completion of the kingdom that awaits us heirs of God, thanks to Jesus Christ's redemptive acts.

+++

In Eucharistic Prayer III, the presider prays words that reflect the concerted effort of the Persons of the Trinity. He declares that all life and holiness issue from the Father, through the Son, and by the working of the Holy Spirit.

Reflection/Discussion

• Which Person of the Trinity do you most often address in prayer? Why?

• How would you rate your relationship with the Holy Spirit on a scale from 1 (non-existent) to 10 (alive and well)?

• When and why have you been in need of a powerful advocate? Perhaps today?

Prayer

O my God, Trinity whom I adore, help me to become utterly forgetful of myself so that I may be established in you, as still and calm as though my soul were already in eternity. Let nothing disturb my peace or make me leave you, O my unchanging God, but at every moment may I penetrate more deeply into the depths of your mystery. Give peace to my soul; make it your heaven, your cherished dwelling and your resting place. May I never leave you there alone, but be wholly present and attentive, wholly alert in my faith, wholly adoring and fully given up to your creative action.

O my beloved Christ, crucified for love, I long to be the bride of your heart. I long to cover you with glory, to love you even unto death! But I sense my weakness and beg you to clothe me with yourself. Identify my soul with all the movements of your soul, submerge me, overwhelm me, possess me, substitute yourself for me, so that my life may become a reflection of your life. Come into me as Adorer, as Restorer, and as Savior.

O Eternal Word, utterance of my God, I want to spend my life listening to you, to become totally teachable so that I might learn all from you. Through all darkness, all emptiness, all powerlessness, I want to keep my eyes fixed on you and to remain in your great light. O my Beloved Star, so fascinate me that I may never be able to leave your radiance.

O Consuming Fire, Spirit of Love, overshadow me so that the Word may be, as it were incarnate again in my soul. May I be for him a new humanity in which he can renew his whole mystery.

And you, O Father, bend lovingly over your poor little creature. Cover her with your shadow, seeing in her only your beloved in whom you are well pleased.

O my Three, my All, my Beatitude, infinite Solitude, Immensity in which I lose myself, I surrender myself to you as your prey. Immerse yourself in me so that I may be immersed in you until I go to contemplate in your light the abyss of your splendor!

~ St. Elizabeth of the Trinity

Action

Whenever I taught the Sign of the Cross to little ones, I encouraged them to make this prayer reverently, not as though they were shooing away flies. Try to pray the Sign of the Cross slowly and conscious of the three Persons you are naming. By this Sign you are not only recalling the death of Jesus that won your salvation, but you are affirming your belief in the Trinity.

2

The Spirit in the Old Testament

Where the Spirit of the Lord is, there is freedom.
~ 2 Corinthians 3:17

The Old Testament contains multiple references to the "spirit" of God. To the Hebrews, this lowercase term stood for the power and action of God—a force, not a person. The human authors of the Old Testament believed that their God, Yahweh, was one. Three persons in God would be akin to heresy for them. God revealed the existence of the Trinity to the human race gradually.

Some people deduce that when God stated, "Let us make humankind in our image, according to our likeness" (Genesis 1:26), the plural pronouns stood for the three divine Persons. Also some assume that in Isaiah's vision of heaven, the triple holy in the angels' proclamation, "Holy, holy, holy is the Lord of hosts" (Isaiah 6:3) hints at the triune God. Both of these are questionable assumptions.

There is no doubt, however, that, beginning with the dawn of creation, the almighty power of God the Holy Spirit was doing marvelous things throughout Old Testament times. And that same life-giving energy is accessible to you today.

The Spirit as Wind

Wind is air, the invisible substance in which we live. A common phrase is "from the Father, through the Son, *in* the Holy Spirit." The Spirit is the "air" in which we meet God.

The Greek word for ruah is *pneuma.* Pneumatology is the study of the Holy Spirit.

The Hebrew word *ruah*, which is feminine, wears three hats: It stands for wind, breath, and spirit. This word appears at the very beginning of the creation story: "The earth was a formless void and darkness covered the face of the deep, while a *wind* from God swept over the face of the waters" (Genesis 1:2). (Other translations have "the spirit of God was hovering over.")

In other Bible stories, wind (the work of the spirit) features as a saving force. To subdue Noah's cataclysmic flood, "God made a wind blow over the earth, and the waters subsided" (Genesis 8:1).

The spirit was also hard at work during the Exodus. One tactic to persuade the Egyptians to free their Israelite slaves was a plague of locusts. These insects were brought into Egypt when the Lord caused an east wind all day and night. (Exodus 10:13) Then they were driven out when the Lord "changed the wind into a very strong west wind" (Exodus 10:19).

When the Israelites, with Egyptians in hot pursuit, were halted at the Red Sea and faced certain doom, God rescued them by means of wind: "The Lord drove the sea back by a strong east wind all night, and turned the sea into dry land; and the waters were divided" (Exodus 14:21). En route to the promised land, as the Israelites trekked through the desert, they were starving. Food was provided when "a wind went out from the Lord, and it brought quails from the sea and let them fall beside the camp" (Numbers 11:31).

The Spirt as Breath

The Bible Walk wax museum in Mansfield, Ohio, houses seventy-eight scenes of life-sized figures. One tableau depicts Jesus raising the deceased daughter of Jairus. After the narrator of the story states Jesus' command, "Little girl, arise," the wax girl's chest begins to rise and fall, startling the museum's visitors.

We need to breathe. Breath is a sign of life. We live until our dying breath. Clearly breath is a good metaphor for the Spirit of God, for he is the giver of life.

The spirit acted to create. After forming the first human's body, God *"breathed* into his nostrils the breath of life; and the man became a living being" (Genesis 2:7). "By the word of the Lord the heavens were made, / and all their host by the *breath* of his mouth" (Psalm 33:6). "When you send forth your spirit, they [all creatures] are created" (Psalm 104:30).

The Holy Spirit participated in the work of creation, keeps it in existence, and continues to guide its unfolding. You have him to thank for your own creation!

In the past, to test for life, someone held a mirror before a person's mouth. If it didn't cloud up, the person was dead.

In 1878 Edwin Hatch of the Church of England wrote the hymn "Breathe on Me, Breath of God." Each of its four verses begins with that invocation.

St. Pope John Paul II wrote an encyclical on the Holy Spirit in 1986. Titled *"Dominum et vivificantem"* (The Lord and Giver of Life), it is on the Holy Spirit in the life of the Church and the world.

In one of the prophet Ezekiel's visions, breath animated a valley full of dry bones. God told him to say: "Come from the four winds, O breath, and breathe upon these slain that they may live," and the bones stood—no doubt an awesome sight! Then God had the prophet foretell a time of national restoration for Israel: "I will put my spirit within you, and you shall live" (Ezekiel 37:9–10, 14).

Dynamic Actions of the Spirit

Besides appearing in the Old Testament in the guise of wind and breath, the spirit is explicitly named quite a few times. Notice that in the following examples, the "spirit" accomplishes the same diverse tasks that the Holy Spirit does for us today.

The spirit imparts knowledge and talents.

- The spirit of God helped the patriarch Joseph to interpret dreams. (Genesis 41:38)
- The "good spirit" instructed the Israelites during the Exodus. (Nehemiah 9:20)
- God said of Bezalel, chief artisan for the Tabernacle and ark of the covenant, "I have filled him with divine spirit, with ability, intelligence, and knowledge in every kind of craft" (Exodus 31:3).

The spirit assists prophets.

- The spirit of God came upon Balaam, and he prophesied blessings for Israel. (Numbers 24:2–3)
- The prophet Isaiah declared, "The spirit of the Lord GOD is upon me, because the LORD has anointed me" (Isaiah 61:1).
- The spirit of God lifted the prophet Ezekiel and set him on his feet to hear God speak. (Ezekiel 2:2)
- The spirit lifted Ezekiel and bore him to the exiles at Tel-abib and to exiles in Chaldea. (Ezekiel 3:14; 11:24)
- Daniel was able to interpret dreams and strange writing on a wall and to solve problems. His enlightenment and wisdom were attributed to a spirit. (Daniel 5:11–16)
- The prophet Micah said, "I am filled with power, with the spirit of the LORD" (Micah 3:8).
- God said, "I will pour out my spirit on all flesh; young sons and your daughters shall prophesy" (Joel 2:28).

The Church established the Holy Spirit as God at the Council of Constantinople in 381 in reaction to the Macedonianism heresy whose "Spirit fighters" denied his divinity.

The spirit inhabited Israel's leaders.

- God told Moses to gather seventy elders of Israel and said, "I will take some of the spirit that is on you and put it on them" (Numbers 11:17).

31

The Book of Judges recounts that the spirit of the Lord began to stir in Samson. Then when the spirit rushed on him, he tore a lion apart and killed thirty men. Again when the spirit rushed on him, ropes binding him fell off.

- Joshua, who took Moses' place in leading the Hebrews into the promised land of Canaan, was described as "a man in whom is the spirit" (Numbers 27:18).
- The spirit came upon Israel's judges and directed their actions: Othniel, Gideon, Jephthah, and Samson.
- Samuel told Saul, the first king of Israel, that the spirit of the LORD would possess him, put him in a prophetic frenzy, and he would become a different person. (1 Samuel 10:6)
- After Samuel anointed David king, "the spirit of the LORD came mightily upon David from that day forward" (1 Samuel 16:13).
- David prayed, "Do not take your holy spirit from me" (Psalm 51:11).

The spirit gives life.

- Isaiah predicted that the wilderness would become fruitful again when "a spirit from on high is poured out" (Isaiah 32:15).
- When God sends forth his spirit, creatures are created and Earth is renewed. (Psalm 104:30)
- In Elihu's speech to Job and his friends, he says, "The spirit of God has made me, and the breath of the Almighty gives me life" (Job 33:4). And, "If he should take back his spirit to himself and gather to himself his breath, all flesh would perish together, and all mortals return to dust" (Job 34:14).

The spirit promotes holiness.

- The psalmist looked to the spirit to become holy: "Teach me to do your will. … Let your good spirit lead me on a level path" (Psalm 143:10).
- God had his prophet say, "I will put my spirit within you, and make you follow my statutes and be careful to observe my ordinances" (Ezekiel 36:27).

When one is speaking of the Holy Spirit, it is just not possible to say enough.

~ Saint Cyril of Jerusalem

It wasn't until New Testament times that the spirit became recognized as Spirit, a Being with intelligence and free will. When Jesus appeared on Earth, the existence of God the Son was revealed. Then Jesus introduced God the Holy Spirit, not as a force or a power of God but as a Person, as you will see in Chapter 4.

Reflection/Discussion

- What is the meaning of spirit as in "class spirit" or "she has spirit"? How is it related to the Old Testament spirit of God?

- What actions of the spirit of God in the Old Testament in particular parallel what you know of the Person of the Holy Spirit?

- Which action of the spirit do you value most?

Prayer

Come, Holy Spirit,
fill the hearts of your faithful
and kindle in them the fire of your love.
Send forth your Spirit
and they shall be created.
And you shall renew the face of the earth.

O, God, who by the light of the Holy Spirit,
did instruct the hearts of the faithful,
grant that by the same Holy Spirit
we may be truly wise and ever enjoy his consolations,
through Christ Our Lord.

Action

We breathe about 28,800 times every twenty-four hours. Make it a habit to pay attention to your breathing for a few minutes each day. During this time, with each breath think of the Holy Spirit filling you with life. This practice will turn your mind to God and bring calm to your days.

3

The Holy Spirit and Jesus

God anointed Jesus of Nazareth
with the Holy Spirit and with power.
~ Acts 10:38

If the life of Jesus were a movie, the Holy Spirit would deserve an award for best supporting actor. He dominates the story of the God-Man on Earth from his conception to his ascension into heaven. On the other hand, if it weren't for Jesus, we might not know that this Third Person existed.

From the Beginning

Because Mary of Nazareth was chosen to be the Mother of God, from the first moment of her existence she was free from original sin, a privilege known as the immaculate conception. This means that Mary was always full of grace—that is, full of divine life. The Trinity, including the Holy Spirit, had made their home in her, directing her daily decisions and always preserving her from sin.

Mary has the title Spouse of the Holy Spirit because of their deep spiritual union.

One day the Angel Gabriel visited Mary and greeted her as "full of grace." Faced with the daunting prospect of becoming the Mother of God, Mary had supernatural help. The gifts of the Holy Spirit she possessed, such as wisdom and fortitude, came into play. She agreed to God's outrageous proposal. The Holy Spirit then came upon Mary, and the power of the Most High overshadowed her. Instantly, with no man's involvement, Jesus was miraculously conceived in her womb.

Through the Spirit's power, God the Son became man to bring new life to the world, establishing a new creation. The incarnation is the prime example of the Spirit uniting divinity with humanity—something he still does in us.

Cloud as Symbol

God "overshadowing" Mary suggests that a cloud is a symbol of the Holy Spirit. A cloud in the Old Testament signified God's saving and protective presence. A pillar of cloud led the Israelites through the desert by day and protected them from the Egyptians at night. A cloud covered Mt. Sinai where Moses met with God and received the Law. Then, too, a cloud settled on the Tent of Meeting and the tabernacle; whenever it lifted, the Israelites knew they were to move on. When Solomon's temple was dedicated, a cloud filled it. At key times during Jesus' life, a cloud also appeared, as you will see in this chapter.

Visitation and Presentation

After agreeing to be the mother of the Son of God, Mary—no doubt prompted by the Holy Spirit—traveled to Judea to assist her elderly relative Elizabeth who was pregnant.

As soon as Elizabeth heard Mary's voice, the Holy Spirit filled her, and she recognized that her young cousin from Nazareth was carrying the Messiah. Elizabeth claimed that the baby in her womb leapt at the sound of Mary's voice. This child was the precursor of Jesus, John the Baptist, and some believe that at this moment he was freed from original sin. This belief is not Church doctrine. However, an angel did reveal to John's father Zechariah, "Even before his birth he will be filled with the Holy Spirit" (Luke 1:15).

Later, Scripture says of John, "the hand of the Lord was with him" (Luke 1:66). The expression "the hand of the Lord" is a title for the Holy Spirit.

The Holy Spirit was at work again at the presentation of the infant Jesus in the temple. This event involved Simeon, a man on whom the Holy Spirit rested. The Spirit let Simeon know that he would not die until he beheld the Messiah. On the day Mary and Joseph brought Jesus to the temple, the Spirit prompted Simeon to go to it. There Simeon was inspired to speak a prophecy concerning Jesus and his mother.

> The hand of the Lord is an apt title for the Holy Spirit because a hand signifies help, comfort, and power.

Preparation for Ministry

In Mark's and Luke's Gospels, the Father addresses Jesus. In Matthew's Gospel, he speaks to the crowd.

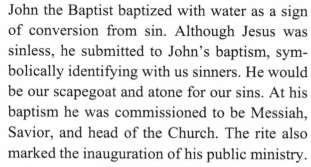

The baptism of Jesus is the first Luminous Mystery of the Rosary.

John the Baptist baptized with water as a sign of conversion from sin. Although Jesus was sinless, he submitted to John's baptism, symbolically identifying with us sinners. He would be our scapegoat and atone for our sins. At his baptism he was commissioned to be Messiah, Savior, and head of the Church. The rite also marked the inauguration of his public ministry.

On this occasion a theophany took place, a manifestation of God. The Holy Spirit in the form of a dove descended on Jesus, and the Father declared Jesus to be his beloved Son in whom he was well pleased. So all three divine Persons were present at the event.

The Holy Spirit equipped Jesus for his mission and inspired all his actions.

Dove as Symbol

A dove stands for the Holy Spirit. At creation the spirit "hovered" over the waters like a bird. Later, after the great flood a dove returned to Noah with an olive branch as a sign that the waters had subsided. That dove heralded a new creation and became a sign of peace. The Spirit as a dove appears in art and poetry, such as Gerard Manley Hopkin's poem "God's Grandeur" in which morning comes "Because the Holy Ghost over the bent / World broods with warm breast and with ah! bright wings."

Previously John the Baptist had foretold that Jesus would baptize "with the Holy Spirit and fire" (Matthew 3:11). The Lord's followers would be immersed in the Holy Spirit. The baptism of fire could refer either to the fiery tongues that came down on the disciples on Pentecost or to the Holy Spirit's purifying work of burning away sin and evil.

Immediately after being baptized, full of the Holy Spirit, Jesus was driven by him into the wilderness. There he lived alone for forty days, fasting and praying. There too, fortified by the Spirit, Jesus successfully stood firm against three temptations that the devil posed. Then angels ministered to him. This lengthy religious ordeal prepared Jesus for his mission, which he would carry out in the constant presence of the Holy Spirit.

Angels (good and bad) are pure spirits, but they are created. The Holy Spirit is uncreated.

Teaching and Healing

Jesus, filled with the power of the Holy Spirit, returned to Galilee and began proclaiming the good news that the kingdom was near and exhorting people to repent. His reputation spread like wildfire. He taught in synagogues, impressing everyone with his knowledge. His neighbors wondered, Isn't this Joseph's son? If only we Christians had a record of Jesus' preaching in those early days!

A chi rho is a symbol for Jesus composed of the first two letters of the Greek word for Christ: chi, *X,* and rho, *P.*

In the Nazareth synagogue Jesus was handed a scroll of the prophet Isaiah. He located a passage pertaining to the Messiah and read it:

> The Spirit of the Lord is upon me,
>   because he has anointed me
>   to bring good news to the poor.
> He has sent me to proclaim release
>   to the captives
>   and recovery of sight to the blind,
>   to let the oppressed go free,
> to proclaim the year of the Lord's favor.
>   (Luke 4:18–19)

Then Jesus declared to the assembly that these words from Isaiah 61:1–2 referred to him. Indeed his ministry, which included preaching and many miracles, was accomplished through the Holy Spirit. In fact, Jesus was given the fullness of the Spirit without measure.

After Pentecost, the apostle Peter preached God's message: "God anointed Jesus of Nazareth with the Holy Spirit and with power" and "he went about doing good and healing all who were oppressed by the devil, for God was with him" (Acts 10:38). Christ, the name we give to Jesus that seems like a surname, actually means "the anointed one." It is a translation of the Hebrew term *messiah.*

People have long been anointed with oil to consecrate them, to set them aside for a special task. Hebrews anointed their prophets, priests, and kings.

You also were anointed with oil at your baptism, for at that time you received a share in the priestly, prophetic, and royal missions of Christ. This oil is chrism, a mixture of olive oil and balsam, which is a fragrant resin. You were anointed with it again at your confirmation. Chrism is used too in the ordination of priests and the consecration of bishops. In addition, objects destined for sacred use—such as altars, patens, and chalices—are anointed.

On Holy Thursday bishops bless the three oils to be used in their parishes: chrism, the oil of catechumens, and the oil of the sick.

Oil as Symbol

Oil symbolizes the Holy Spirit for several reasons. It heals. Recall how the Samaritan poured oil on the beaten man's wounds. Today CBD oil as medicine is growing in popularity. Holy oil is used in the Anointing of the Sick, when the Holy Spirit imparts the grace to face sickness and death with courage and peace. Burned in lamps, oil gives light. The Holy Spirit dispels the darkness of our minds. In the United States oil is the largest provider of energy. Likewise, the Holy Spirit provides us with power. Also oil lubricates, as in WD-40. Oil—especially scented oil—comforts, soothes, and relaxes. It's used during massages. For centuries athletes have been rubbed with oil to strengthen and limber them up. You were anointed with oil in the sacrament of Confirmation as a sign of the strength the Spirit gives you to run the race of life.

Joy is the echo of God's life within us.

~ Blessed Abbot Columba Marmion, O.S.B.

God gave Moses the stone tablets of Law "written with the finger of God" (Exodus 31:18).

The Holy Spirit is the oil of gladness. After seventy disciples returned from ministering successfully, Jesus "rejoiced in the Holy Spirit" (Luke 10:21). Because the Spirit dwells in your heart, you can experience a deep-down joy no one can take from you.

The Holy Spirit guided Jesus as he chose the twelve apostles and as he decided where and to whom to minister. The words Jesus spoke—his sermons, Beatitudes, and parables—were inspired by the Spirit. Jesus claimed, "He whom God sent speaks the words of God, for he gives the Spirit without measure" (Matthew 3:34).

Jesus also performed exorcisms through the Holy Spirit. When accused of casting out demons by Beelzebul, the ruler of demons, Jesus implied that he performed exorcisms by the Spirit of God. He stated, "If it is by the Spirit of God that I cast out demons, then the kingdom of God has come to you" (Matthew 12:28). Instead of "the Spirit of God" Luke 11:20 has "finger of God," another title for the Third Person, referring to his divine touch.

At Jesus' Transfiguration when his glory was revealed, a bright cloud overshadowed the three apostles who witnessed the event. From it came the voice of God the Father, acknowledging that Jesus was his Son. The cloud symbolized the presence of the Spirit. Therefore, this event paralleled the theophany of the Trinity that occurred at the baptism of Jesus.

Death and Resurrection

The Holy Spirit made possible the redemptive sacrifice of Jesus. Scripture says that Jesus offered himself upon the cross—like a lamb without spot or blemish—through the power of the Holy Spirit. (Hebrews 9:14).

The astonishing resurrection of Jesus was also due to the energy of the Holy Spirit—and so will your resurrection be: "If the Spirit of him who raised Jesus from the dead dwells in you, he who raised Christ from the dead will give life to your mortal bodies also through his Spirit that dwells in you" (Romans 8:11).

After Jesus rose from the dead and before he ascended, he instructed the disciples through the ministry of the Holy Spirit. (Acts 1:2) He ordered them to baptize all nations "in the name of the Father and of the Son and of the Holy Spirit" (Matthew 28:19). Then he was lifted up and a cloud took him away. Now Jesus is seated at the Father's right hand.

The Holy Spirit was an animator and driving force throughout Jesus' sojourn on Earth until he returned to heaven.

After Jesus was glorified, he "received from the Father the promise of the Holy Spirit" and the Spirit's power was poured out on the infant Church. (Acts 2:33) So, Jesus did not leave us orphans. The Holy Spirit is the presence of the risen Jesus. It could be said that the purpose of

In the Communion Rite of the Mass, the priest may address Jesus and say, "by the will of the Father *and work of the Holy Spirit* your death brought life to the world."

43

Peristeria, or the "flower of the Holy Spirit," is an orchid that has white flowers whose centers resemble a dove. It is the national flower of Panama.

the incarnation was the sending of the Spirit who would lead humankind back to the Father.

At the end of time, Jesus will return, coming on clouds no less. (Mark 13:26; Revelation 1:7) Then the faithful will be one with Father, Son, and Holy Spirit.

Reflection/Discussion

• What are some amazing healings that Jesus performed when he was filled with the Spirit?

• When have you experienced a triumph that you could credit to the Holy Spirit's help?

Prayer

Glory be to the Father, and to the Son, and to the Holy Spirit. As it was in the beginning, is now, and ever shall be, world without end. Amen.

Action

Spend a few minutes pondering one miracle that Jesus accomplished with the assistance of the Holy Spirit. Are you or someone you care for in need of a miracle? Invoke the Holy Spirit's help.

4

Jesus' Teachings about the Holy Spirit

Through the Holy Spirit we are restored to paradise,
led back to the Kingdom of heaven, and adopted as children,
given liberty to call God "Father" and to share
in Christ's grace, called children of light,
and given a share in eternal glory.
~ St. Basil, *De Spiritu Sancto*, #36

At Confirmation the candidates receive a strengthening of the Holy Spirit and his gifts. As part of their preparation for this sacrament, they are instructed about the Spirit and his roles. Similarly, before the apostles received the Holy Spirit, Jesus informed them about this Third Person.

Introduction of the Holy Spirit

John's Gospel presents Jesus' comprehensive lesson on the Holy Spirit in the context of the Last Supper. On the night before his death, Jesus broke the sad news to his disciples that he was about to return to his Father. But his going would make

St. John of the Cross wrote in his poem *Spiritual Canticle,* "Soul, most beautiful of all creatures, so anxious to know the dwelling place of your Beloved [God] in order to go in search of him and be united with him, ... you yourself are his dwelling."

it possible for the Holy Spirit to come to them. Following are concepts Jesus taught about this Third Person that evening.

The Holy Spirit lives within us forever as a helper.

"I will ask the Father, and he will give you another Advocate, to be with you forever. This is the Spirit of truth, whom the world cannot receive, because it neither sees him nor knows him. You know him, because he abides with you, and he will be in you" (John 14:16–17).

Lines in James Taylor's song "You've Got a Friend" could easily be spoken by the Holy Spirit: "When you're down and troubled and you need a helping hand, . . . Close your eyes and think of me" and "All you got to do is call and I'll be there."

At your baptism the Trinity entered you, a mystery known as the divine indwelling. From that instant the Holy Spirit became your constant guest and intimate friend. St. Paul wrote, "Do you not know that you are God's temple and that God's Spirit dwells in you?" (1 Corinthians 3:16). You should never feel lonely. All through your life until your last breath the Spirit will be living and active in the depths of your soul as a powerful partner.

—

Call on the Holy Spirit for help, especially before undertaking something of importance. You can be assured of assistance. After all, the Spirit is God, he is faithful, and he has a deep love for you—more than anyone on Earth has. Any failing on your part, no matter how grievous, is no deterrent to him.

Notice that Jesus coined a name for this Third Person: Spirit of truth. While different philosophies and religions vie for your attention, you can look to the Holy Spirit to give you a true understanding of the things of God and spiritual matters. With his enlightenment you discern truth from falsehood and what is good from what is evil. You set your heart not on things of the Earth but on heavenly things. Your values are in sync with those of Jesus.

To set the mind on the flesh is death, but to set the mind on the Spirit is life and peace.

~ Romans 8:6

Flesh here does not refer to the body, which is good, but to sin—anything opposed to God. Richard Rohr, O.F.M., suggests substituting ego for *flesh*.

The Holy Spirit teaches us and reminds us of what Jesus taught.

"The Advocate, the Holy Spirit, whom the Father will send in my name, will teach you everything, and remind you of all that I have said to you" (John 14:26).

Jesus had not taught the disciples all they needed to know. He admitted, "I still have many things to say to you, but you cannot bear them now" (John 16:12). The Spirit continued

The Holy Spirit is called the living memory of the Church.

the disciples' lessons and kept the teachings of Jesus fresh in their minds.

The Holy Spirit also helps you to know and understand the truths of our faith. He gives insights through books and other media, homilies, chance meetings with other people, and personal experiences. Sometimes the Spirit whispers in the silence of your heart as you pray. During the course of the day, something Jesus said might cross your mind. For instance, maybe as you contemplate purchasing a superfluous item, you recall his parable about the man who intended to build bigger barns to store his abundant crops instead of sharing them with the poor—but then died that day.

The Holy Spirit witnesses to Jesus.

"When the Advocate comes, who I will send to you from the Father, the Spirit of truth who comes from the Father, he will testify on my behalf" (John 15:26).

Jesus revealed the Father, and the Holy Spirit reveals Jesus. The Spirit confirms and strengthens your faith in Jesus Christ. He helps you hold fast to the truths that Jesus is the Son of God and our saving Lord. People may criticize your beliefs and argue with you about them. With the Spirit's assistance you can stand firm against doubts and pressures that threaten to weaken your faith. You can keep Jesus—and Jesus alone—at the center of your life. Furthermore, you can allow the Spirit to witness through you not only by defending your faith but by sharing it with others.

Elsewhere in Scripture Jesus assured his followers that when they were brought before authorities for their belief in him, they were not to worry about how to defend themselves. The Holy Spirit would teach them what they were to say. (Luke 12:11–12)

The Holy Spirit helps us to realize the truth about Jesus.

St. Peter Favre, S.J., habitually prayed, "Heavenly Father, give me your Spirit." He said that at the age of twelve the Holy Spirit inspired him to consecrate his life to God.

"If I do not go away, the Advocate will not come to you; but if I go, I will send him to you. And when he comes, he will prove the world wrong about sin [convict the world of sin] and righteousness and judgment; about sin, because they do not believe in me; about righteousness, because I am going to the Father and you will see me no longer; about judgment, because the ruler of this world has been condemned" (John 16:7–11).

Jesus was rejected by many people in his world: religious and secular leaders as well as the followers who abandoned him. They could

Pontius Pilate asked Jesus, "What is truth?" Previously Jesus had said, "I am the way, the truth, and the life."

not accept that he was the Messiah. After Jesus was glorified, he sent the Spirit to reveal that those who did not accept him had sinned. He was proved righteous, and those earthly rulers who condemned him were condemned themselves. Temptations to doubt truths about Jesus, such as his divinity or his presence in the Eucharist, can be blown away by the Holy Spirit. He was sent to lead us safe and sound back to the Father.

The Holy Spirit reveals truths.

"When the Spirit of truth comes, he will guide you into all the truth; for he will not speak on his own, but will speak whatever he hears, and he will declare to you the things that are to come. He will glorify me, because he will take what is mine and declare it to you. All that the Father has is mine. For this reason I said that he will take what is mine and declare it to you" (John 16:13–14).

Some of Jesus' teachings mystified the disciples. But then the Holy Spirit enlightened them, just as he does our church leaders today. St. Paul acknowledged that the wisdom he himself imparted was from the Spirit (1 Corinthians 2:12–13). Your grasp of the eternal verities—limited though it may be—is due to the Spirit as well. Whenever you yearn to deepen your understanding of life or the faith, turn to the Holy Spirit. You can trust him to reveal the truth because he is one with the Father and the Son.

When Jesus taught, people were astounded. They asked, "Where did this man get all this? What is this wisdom that has been given to him?" (Mark 6:2).

The Spirit at work in Jesus was also at work in saints. Great doctors of the Church like St. Ambrose, St. Anselm, St. Augustine, and St. Teresa of Avila taught and wrote about the faith in a masterful way. Then there was St. Julie Billiart (1751–1816), a peasant girl in France who had very little education but possessed an uncanny knowledge of spiritual things. Hearing of her gift, a bishop called Julie in to test her before a group of priests. When she answered their questions successfully, they all marveled at her grasp of theological concepts.

The Holy Spirit guides the Church in developing doctrine. One case in point is the fourth-century Nicene Creed that clarified that Jesus and the Spirit were divine.

Furthermore, the Spirit reveals things to come: "No prophecy ever came by human will, but men and women moved by the Holy Spirit spoke from God" (2 Peter 1:21).

What Jesus was for the apostles, the Holy Spirit is for us.

The Spirit led the Church to proclaim two relatively recent dogmas: the Immaculate Conception in 1954 and the Assumption of Mary in 1950.

Previous Teachings of Jesus about the Holy Spirit

The chaplet (rosary) of the Holy Spirit was approved by Pope Leo XIII in 1902. Directions for praying it are on page 121. Another chaplet was composed by Blessed Elena Guerra in 1896, asking for a new Pentecost and invoking the seven gifts. It can be found on the Internet.

No doubt moved by the Spirit, the Pharisee Nicodemus came to see Jesus at night, and Jesus gave him a private lesson. He taught that to enter God's kingdom it is necessary to be born again, this time of water and the Spirit. At this rebirth through the Holy Spirit, sin is obliterated and we have new, eternal life.

Also prior to the Last Supper, Jesus assured us: "If you who are evil [meaning sinful], know how to give good gifts to your children, how much more will the heavenly Father give the Holy Spirit to those who ask him!" (Luke 11:13). Parents like to give gifts to their children. The Holy Spirit is a special gift from our loving Father—a gift par excellence. The Spirit is someone who brings you great delight and peace. He is also an agent who enables you to walk with God and live by God's standards. Jesus teaches that the Spirit will be given more fully to those who ask the Father for him. This should encourage you to ask regularly for the Holy Spirit to come to your assistance.

The Holy Spirit already came to you at your baptism and confirmation, and he will increase his action on your behalf at times when you ask his help. Or he may come unbidden when you need him and his spiritual gifts as he did for Nicodemus.

I witnessed the strange workings of the Spirit one day when I made a phone call. A man answered, and I identified myself as Sister Kathleen. He said, "You have the wrong number. But I was just sitting here asking God for a sign that he existed. Your call confirmed it for me." Both of us were dumbfounded.

Jesus made a puzzling statement: "Whoever blasphemes against the Holy Spirit will not be forgiven" (Luke 12:10). Scripture scholars take this to refer to people who totally reject Jesus and his message. The Spirit testifies to Jesus. Therefore, those who refuse to accept Jesus as Lord and Savior insult the Holy Spirit. Their eternal life is in jeopardy.

Another time, Jesus verified that the Spirit was operating during Old Testament times. He declared that King David, who wrote many of the psalms, spoke "by the Holy Spirit" (Mark 12:36).

Among Cathedrals named for the Holy Spirit are those in Istanbul, Turkey; Bismarck, North Dakota; Albuquerque, New Mexico; Minsk, Belarus; Denpasar, Indonesia; and Accra, Ghana.

Water and the Holy Spirit

Jesus obliquely mentioned the Holy Spirit during the eight-day Jewish feast of Tabernacles. On each day of that feast, the priest filled a golden pitcher with water and then led a procession to the Temple. There at the altar he poured the water along with a vessel of wine into a silver basin.

"Living" water is flowing water like in a river, stream or fountain as opposed to water in a well or cistern.

On the last day of this feast, Jesus cried out, "Let anyone who is thirsty come to me, and let the one who believes in me drink. As Scripture says, 'Out of the believer's heart shall flow rivers of living water' " (John 7:37–38). The evangelist explained, "Now he said this about the Spirit, which believers in him were to receive" (John 7:39).

That was not the first time Jesus referred to the Spirit as living water. When he encountered the Samaritan woman at the well, he told her that he could have given her living water. He said, "Those who drink of the water that I will give them will never be thirsty. The water that I will give will become in them a spring of water gushing up to eternal life" (John 4:14).

On the cross when the spear pierced the side of Jesus, blood and water flowed out. Often the sacred blood is said to symbolize the Eucharist and the sacred water, the sacrament of Baptism. The flow is also regarded as the birth of the Church, comparable to the story of a rib taken from a sleeping Adam's side to form Eve. Some scholars, however, view the water issuing from Jesus at the site of our salvation as a metaphor for the Holy Spirit. He is the river of life that renews creation. Flowing from the side of Christ when his atoning sacrifice was complete, the Spirit was let loose on humankind.

Water appears again in John's vision of heaven: "Then the angel showed me the river of the water of life, bright as crystal, flowing from the throne of God and of the Lamb [Jesus]" (Revelation 22:1). Notice that here water originates from the Father and the Son just as the Spirit does.

St. Paul makes use of the water metaphor in teaching that church members are united in one body. He says, "We were all made to drink of one Spirit" (1 Corinthians 12:13). He again likens the Spirit to water when he writes to an early church leader, "This Spirit he poured on us richly through Jesus Christ our Savior" (Titus 3:6).

The psalmist compares our longing for God to thirsting: "As a deer longs for flowing streams, so my soul longs for you, O God" (Psalm 42:1) and "My soul thirsts for you" (Psalm 63:1).

Water as Symbol

As an image for the Holy Spirit, water is an excellent choice. Comparing the Holy Spirit to water points to his life-giving power. All living things need water to live and to grow. We humans, who are mostly composed of water, can live only about three days without it. Similarly, the Holy Spirit is the source and sustainer of your spiritual life. Your earthly life began in water in your mother's womb, and your divine life originated with the waters of Baptism.

Besides being necessary for life, water cleanses and refreshes, both functions of the Holy Spirit, who wipes out sin and renews hearts. He quenches our thirst for God and meaning in our lives.

Gift of Peace

Scripture defines the kingdom of God as "righteous- ness and peace and joy in the Holy Spirit" (Romans 14:17).

On the day of the Resurrection, Jesus gave his apostles a special gift for the Church. That evening he appeared to them in the upper room and greeted, "Peace be with you." After show- ing them his wounds, he repeated the greeting and said, "As the Father has sent me, so I send you." He breathed on them and said, "Receive the Holy Spirit." (John 20:19–22). These words were symbolic, a promise that the Spirit would come; for he would only come upon the dis- ciples personally and in fullness on Pentecost after Jesus had ascended to heaven and been glorified.

Then Jesus gave the disciples the authority and the power to forgive sins. Through them the Spirit would forgive sins and bring peace to our troubled consciences. God's forgiveness is extended in the sacraments of Baptism, Recon- ciliation, Eucharist, and Anointing of the Sick.

Today you can trust that the priest or bishop who hears your confession in the sacrament of Reconciliation is provided with light given by the Holy Spirit.

When Jesus returned to his Father in heaven, he placed the care of his Church in the hands of the Holy Spirit. Our Christian faith depends on the Spirit. St. Paul taught, "No one can say 'Jesus is Lord' except by the Holy Spirit" (1 Corinthians 12:3).

Reflection/Discussion

• When have you been inspired by the Holy Spirit? Did you have an insight about the faith? Be prompted to act?

• Did anyone challenge your faith? How did you respond?

• How might you witness to Jesus? To whom?

Prayer

O Holy Spirit, beloved of my soul, I adore you.
Enlighten me, guide me, strengthen me, console me.
Tell me what I should do and command me to do it.
I promise to submit myself to all that you desire of me
    and to accept all that you permit to happen to me.
Only show me what is your will.

~ Cardinal Mercier

Action

One form of prayer is simply loving attention to God abiding within us. It is going to the depths of our being and focusing quietly on God's presence there. This prayer is called centering prayer because during it we are centered exclusively on God. Experience at least five minutes of this silent prayer method. Here is how to do it:

—

First choose a sacred word or phrase that you will use to call your attention back if it wanders. Then sit comfortably with your eyes closed and quiet down. Think only of God living deep within you. Be present to him and his overwhelming love and goodness. Rest in his presence.

Whenever you are aware of things other than God, use your prayer word to bring you back, like a tug on a kite string. Focus on giving God your loving attention.

5

The Holy Spirit and the Church

*The Holy Spirit, whom Christ the head pours out
on his members, builds, animates, and sanctifies the Church.*
~ Catechism of the Catholic Church, #747

A teacher was giving her first graders a tour of the church. She pointed to the large stained-glass window depicting Pentecost. "See the Holy Spirit coming upon Mary and the apostles," she said. One little girl piped up, "Where are you?"

Neither the teacher nor anyone of us was present when the Holy Spirit came to the Church for the first time. But he did come down upon us church members at our baptism and then strengthened his life in us at our confirmation.

Religious time can be viewed as unfolding in three stages. First came the age of the Father presented in the Old Testament, followed by the age of the Son described in the Gospels. The age of the Holy Spirit was inaugurated at Pentecost in the first century, extends through the present, and continues on into the future until the Second Coming.

The Acts of the Apostles is a record of the early years of this last age. The book is fairly bursting with accounts showing the Spirit alive and active in the first Christians.

Pentecost

One name for the Acts of the Apostles is the Book of the Holy Spirit.

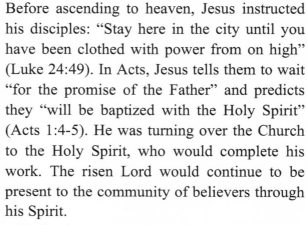

To Hebrews the number seven stood for completeness or perfection. Fifty is seven times seven plus one, signifying a superabundance.

Before ascending to heaven, Jesus instructed his disciples: "Stay here in the city until you have been clothed with power from on high" (Luke 24:49). In Acts, Jesus tells them to wait "for the promise of the Father" and predicts they "will be baptized with the Holy Spirit" (Acts 1:4-5). He was turning over the Church to the Holy Spirit, who would complete his work. The risen Lord would continue to be present to the community of believers through his Spirit.

Following Jesus' directions, the disciples and his mother, Mary, gathered in an upper room in Jerusalem where they prayed for nine days. Then on Pentecost, a Jewish harvest feast that occurred fifty days after Passover, the "power from on high" descended on them. In the story of Pentecost, the Holy Spirit's arrival was accompanied by two natural phenomena. The sound of violent wind roared through the house where the disciples were. A flame of fire—like the glory of God—rested above the head of each one.

The Spirit had brought Jesus to life in the womb of the Virgin Mary. On Pentecost he brought the Church, the mystical body of Jesus, to life. His mission was to carry on the work of Christ, finishing the work of creation and bringing it to its fulfillment.

Wind as Symbol

Recall that wind was present at creation, dried up the Great Flood, and rescued the Israelites during the Exodus. Wind, which is invisible, can be powerful, as in tornadoes and hurricanes, or gentle and soothing as summer breezes that bring relief on a hot day. Wind drives windmills that generate electricity and pump water. It causes joy by pushing sailboats and flying kites. These aspects of wind are also true of the Holy Spirit. Unseen, he is powerful yet gentle; he makes life easier for us and brings us joy.

Fire as Symbol

Fire is associated with God. As God established a covenant with Abram, a flaming torch appeared (Genesis 15:17). God spoke to Moses from a burning bush and came down on Mt. Sinai in fire (Exodus 19:18). Fire is powerful and useful. It cooks food, provides warmth and light, and purifies gold and silver. Fire can be life-giving. Sequoias are regenerated when fire releases their seeds. Moreover, fire is beautiful and comforting whether in candle flames, in fireplaces, or at campsites. Fire's features are comparable to those of the Holy Spirit. The Spirit is a powerful helper; he enlightens, purifies, and gives spiritual life, saving us from eternal fire. St. Paul refers to the Spirit as fire, warning, "Do not quench the Holy Spirit" (1 Thessalonians 5:19). The mystic poem of St. John of the Cross about union with God is called "Living Flame of Love."

Effects of the Spirit

In an Old Testament story, people undertook to build a city and a tower to reach heaven for their own glory. God stopped them by making them speak different languages and sending them all over the world. Their city was named Babel.

Pentecost undid Babel. People from many nations understood the apostles. The Spirit brought about unity.

Previously the apostles lacked understanding and faith. After the multiplication of loaves and fish, Jesus rebuked them, "Do you not yet understand?" (Mark 8:21). Neither did they believe the reports of the resurrection from Mary Magdalene and the two disciples who met the risen Jesus on the way to Emmaus. Furthermore, all but one apostle had deserted Jesus and fled for their lives after he was captured. But now, filled with the Holy Spirit, courageously the apostles came forth from the house where they had been hiding and began preaching the Good News about Jesus. They spoke so enthusiastically that on seeing them observers assumed they were drunk.

People from different countries had come to Jerusalem to celebrate Pentecost, one of the three major Jewish feasts. Remarkably, although they spoke various languages, all were able to understand the apostles. Peter told them to repent and be baptized so that their sins would be forgiven and they too would "receive the gift of the Holy Spirit" (Acts 2:38).

The apostles went on to perform astounding deeds and persuaded thousands to believe in Jesus. Empowered by the Holy Spirit, Peter cured a beggar lame from birth so completely that the man jumped up and went walking and leaping to the temple. (Acts 3:1–10)

At the temple, Peter and John were arrested for preaching about Jesus. Peter, filled with the Holy Spirit and with the cured man beside him, addressed the religious leaders. They were amazed because the two apostles were "uneducated and ordinary men" (Acts 4:13). Jesus had promised that when the apostles were brought before authorities because of their faith, the Holy Spirit would give them words to speak. And that is exactly what happened.

The Descent of the Holy Spirit on the Apostles is the third Glorious Mystery of the Rosary.

The Holy Spirit Comes to Others

The Spirit was not confined to the apostles. When a group of believers prayed for boldness in speaking, the place where they were shook, and they were filled with the Holy Spirit. They then boldly spoke the word of God. (Acts 4:29–31)

The deacon Stephen, too, was strengthened by the Holy Spirit. His preaching led to false accusations, and he was hauled before the high priest and council. He preached to them and bluntly told them they were opposing the Holy Spirit and had murdered the Messiah. While the religious leaders fumed, Stephen was filled with the Holy Spirit and beheld a vision of Jesus standing at God's right hand. Then Stephen was stoned to death, making him the first Christian martyr (witness). (Acts 7:54–60)

Another deacon, Philip, also benefited from the Spirit's assistance in evangelizing. The Spirit sent him to the chariot of an Ethiopian eunuch who was reading the prophet Isaiah and not understanding it. After Philip baptized the man, the Spirit "snatched Philip away" to preach in other towns. (Acts 8:26–40)

Evangelizing Gentiles

The Holy Spirit saw to it that the Church welcomed people beyond Jews. When Peter and John laid their hands on Samaritans—longtime enemies of the Jews—they received the Holy Spirit. (Acts 8:14–17) Throughout Israel, the Church increased in number, "living in the fear of the Lord and in the comfort of the Holy Spirit" (Acts 9:31).

One day, prompted by a dream, Peter proclaimed the Good News to Cornelius, who was a Roman centurion, and the man's household. As he did so, the Holy Spirit fell upon them and they spoke in tongues and praised God. This convinced Peter to baptize the Gentiles. (Acts 10:44–48).

Other disciples proclaimed the Lord Jesus to Gentiles, Greeks in Antioch. "The hand of the Lord" (name for the Holy Spirit) was with them, and many people became believers. (Acts 11:20–21)

Saul (also called Paul) became the apostle to the Gentiles. Once a zealous persecutor of Christians, Saul was converted when he was on the way to arrest Christians. He encountered the risen Jesus and was struck blind. Jesus sent Ananias to Saul so that he would regain his sight, be baptized, and "be filled with the Holy Spirit" (Acts 9:17). The Spirit clearly directed Saul's missionary activity:

Saul credits the Holy Spirit's power for winning over the Gentiles. (Romans 15:18–19) He once wrote to his converts that he needed no letter of recommendation because they were "a letter of Christ, ... written not with ink but with the Spirit of the living God" (2 Corinthians 3:3).

- The Spirit sent Barnabas and Saul from Antioch to preach in Cyprus. There Saul, filled with the Holy Spirit, chided a false prophet and predicted he would be blind for a while. (Acts 13:1–11)
- When Paul and Barnabas were persecuted and driven from Antioch, they "were filled with joy and with the Holy Spirit" (Acts 13:50–52).
- Paul and others were "forbidden by the Holy Spirit to speak the word in Asia." Then when they attempted to go into Bithynia, "the Spirit of Jesus did not allow them" (Acts 16:6–7).
- In Ephesus, Paul met about twelve disciples who had only undergone John's baptism of repentance. They hadn't heard of the Holy Spirit. Paul baptized them in Jesus' name. "When Paul had laid hands on them, the Holy Spirit came upon them, and they spoke in tongues and prophesied" (Acts 19:1–7).

- "Paul resolved in the Spirit to go through Macedonia and Achaia, and then to go on to Jerusalem" (Acts 19:21).

Prophecy

The Spirit's gift of prophecy was evident in the early Church. Agabus "predicted by the Spirit that there would be a severe famine over all the world" (Acts 11:28). Later the Holy Spirit through him foretold that the Jews in Jerusalem would bind Paul and hand him over to the Gentiles. (Acts 21:10–11) At Antioch "there were prophets and teachers" (Acts 13:1). And in Caesarea, Philip had "four unmarried daughters who had the gift of prophecy" (Acts 21:9).

Laying on of Hands

Notice that the apostles laid hands on people who were becoming Christian. They did this to invoke the power of the Holy Spirit. This imposition of hands is an essential part of two sacraments today. In Confirmation, it occurs as the bishop anoints with chrism. It also takes place during the ordination of deacons, priests, and bishops. Laying on of hands also happens during a baptism but is not considered the matter of this sacrament.

Role in the Church

The Holy Spirit permeates the Church and empowers her to carry on the mission of Jesus. He forms the Church, organizes it, and vivifies it. The solid structure of the Church can be ascribed to the gifts he bestows on individuals and on the community (as described in chapter nine).

Where the Church is, there is also the Spirit of God, and where the Spirit of God is, there are also the Church and all grace.

~ Saint Irenaeus

Because of the Holy Spirit, the Church is one, holy, catholic (universal), and apostolic. He ensures that the tradition that originated with the apostles is preserved, and he protects the Church from heresies by overseeing her teachings and decisions.

The Spirit plays a role in choosing church leaders. Speaking to the elders at Ephesus, Paul said, "Keep watch over yourselves and over all the flock, of which the Holy Spirit has made you overseers, to shepherd the church of God" (Acts 20:28). For good reason on the first day of a conclave to elect a new pope, as well as at the opening of ecumenical councils, the hymn "Veni, Creator Spiritus" is sung, imploring the guidance of the Holy Spirit. The Spirit directs church leaders as they govern and keeps them from error.

The Holy Spirit also guided the Church in establishing the rituals for the seven sacraments and through all of them imparts grace, the divine life won by Jesus' Paschal Mystery.

—

Like the stones of a temple, cut for a building of God the Father, you have been lifted up to the top by the crane of Jesus Christ, which is the cross, and the cable of the Holy Spirit.

~ Saint Ignatius of Antioch

St. Cyril of Jerusalem wrote that the Holy Spirit is with us "to defend and sanctify the Church, as a guide for souls and a helmsman for storm-tossed humankind, a light to guide the wayfarers, a judge who presides over the contest and the crowning of the victorious."

The Spirit is the source of unity in the Church, making us a community. This bond of love in the Trinity is also the bond between Christ and us and the bond that makes all of us one. He is also operating in the ecumenical movement whose goal is to unite all Christians. The Spirit's work is not limited to Catholics but to all people of good will.

The Holy Spirit inspires us to spread the word about Jesus just as he did the apostles. St. Patrick revealed the reason why he went to Ireland in his *Confession:* "I am bound to the Spirit and it is not I, but the Lord who asked me to come. Was it without God or according to the flesh that I came to Ireland? Who drove me here—bound by the Spirit—to see no one related to me?"

A metaphor for the Church is the bride of Christ. Our ultimate goal is union with Christ celebrated at the marriage feast of heaven. Therefore, we anticipate his coming at the end of time. The Spirit is one with us as we pray for this Second Coming. This is expressed in the last book of the Bible: "The Spirit and the bride say, 'Come' " (Revelation 22:17).

In 1972, St. Pope Paul VI identified the Holy Spirit as the greatest need of the Church:

> [It is the Holy Spirit] who animates and sanctifies the Church, who is her divine breath, the wind in her sail, the principle of her unity, the inner source of her light and strength, her support and consoler, the source of her charisms and songs, her peace and joy, the pledge and prelude of her blessed and eternal life.

Anyone who does not have the Spirit of Christ does not belong to him.

~ Ephesians 8:9

The Holy Spirit continues the salvific work of Jesus. He helps the Church shape the Good News in keeping with the signs of the times. Down through the centuries he brings forth new movements: monasticism, religious orders like the Franciscans, lay communities, and associations like Sant'Egidio and the Catholic Worker Movement, and programs like Cursillo and Marriage Encounter. He guides councils and synods like the Amazon Synod. Nowadays the Spirit operates through social media, evangelizing the world and unifying believers.

In God's great design, the Spirit is the life-force that draws us nearer to God, assists us in communicating with and worshiping God, and makes it possible for us to know Jesus as Lord and Savior. The Spirit is required for salvation, which is attainable because Jesus died and rose in the power of the Holy Spirit.

Reflection/Discussion

The Holy Spirit is the bridge between God and the world.

• Where have you witnessed the Spirit alive and well in the Church?

• What new movements in the Church or in the world appear to be inspired by the Spirit?

• How do you or can you support the work of missionaries?

Prayer

Divine Spirit, renew your wonders in this our age as in a new Pentecost, and grant that your Church, praying perseveringly and insistently with one heart and mind together with Mary, the Mother of Jesus, and guided by Blessed Peter, may increase the reign of the Divine Savior, the reign of truth and justice, the reign of love and peace. Amen.

~ St. Pope John XXIII
Prayer to convoke Vatican Council II

Action

Plan and then carry out a way you can evangelize with the help of the Holy Spirit. You might assist with your parish RCIA program, teach a religion class, or invite someone to church with you.

6

The Holy Spirit and Scripture

*I believe that the intention of Holy Writ
was to persuade men of the truths
necessary to salvation;
such as neither science nor other means
could render credible,
but only the voice of the Holy Spirit.*
~ Galileo Galilei

Scripture has power to impact our lives through the Holy Spirit. It's said that St. Francis of Assisi opened the Bible three times and each time found a guiding principle for the Franciscan Holy Rule. St. Augustine in his book *Confessions* attributed his conversion to Scripture. He heard a child singing, "Take and read," and picked up a Bible. It opened to Romans 13:13–14 where he read: "Let us live honorably as in the day, not in revelry and drunkenness, not in debauchery and licentiousness, not in quarreling and jealousy. Instead put on the Lord Jesus Christ, and make no provision for the flesh." When Thomas Merton was discerning whether to join the Trappists, known for their silence, he, too, sought God's will

In 2019, Pope Francis established the Third Sunday of Ordinary Time as the Sunday of God's Word.

in Scripture. His random opening led him to the words "Be still" from Psalm 46:10.

Quite a few times I have found direction, comfort, and encouragement when I turned to Scripture. Perhaps the most striking experience occurred during the exodus from convents during the sixties. Shortly after I entered, I was in chapel asking Jesus if I should leave too. I walked up to the open Bible, and my eyes fell on these words: "Everyone who has left houses or brothers or sisters or father or mother or children or fields, for my name's sake, will receive a hundredfold, and will inherit eternal life" (Matthew 19:27). I stayed. That clearly was God's plan for me.

Roles of the Holy Spirit

Scripture is the Word of God in the words of human beings. It is living and active (Hebrews 4:12). In the apostolic letter in which Pope Francis established the Sunday of God's Word, he wrote, "Sacred Scripture, by the working of the Holy Spirit, makes human words written in human fashion become the word of God."

The Holy Spirit played a prominent part in the development this Holy Book and continues to be involved in it. Through him, God's Word speaks to every culture and every generation. The Bible is a classic.

Authoring the Bible

First, the Holy Spirit influenced the minds of those believers who wrote Scripture. Because he inspired them to write the truths God wanted to communicate to us for our salvation, he is the primary author. According to the Second Vatican Council, "Sacred Scripture is the speech of God as it is put down in writing under the breath of the Holy Spirit" (*Deo Verbum*, 9).

The Spirit's authorship of the Bible is supported by Scripture in several places. A group of early Christians acknowledged in a prayer that David wrote the psalms by the Holy Spirit. (Acts 4:24–26) And Paul once declared to Jewish leaders that the Holy Spirit spoke through the prophet Isaiah. (Acts 28:25–27) Scripture further attests that "no prophecy ever came by human will, but men and women moved by the Holy Spirit spoke from God" (2 Peter 1:21).

All Scripture is inspired by God and is useful for teaching, for reproof, for correction and for training in righteousness.

~ 2 Timothy 3:16

The word translated "inspired" literally is "God-breathed."

Forming the Canon

Second, the Holy Spirit guided the Church in determining which books would be included in the canon, the books officially recognized as divinely inspired. The third-century Greek version, the Septuagint, was accepted as the Old Testament rather than the

—

Scriptures wish to be read through the very Spirit with which they were written; and they must be understood through this method.

~ William of Saint-Thierry

St. Benedict's Rule recommends listening "with the ear of your heart." That is also good advice for reading Scripture.

Hebrew version, which excluded some books. As for the New Testament, among the texts circulating, the Spirit led the Church to approve the books currently in Scripture. For example, the Gospel of John was accepted as Sacred Scripture but not the Gospel of Thomas or the Protoevangelium of St. James.

Helping Us to Understand Scripture

Third, the Holy Spirit works in us through Scripture. Some Bibles included a prayer to the Holy Spirit on a front page. Even if your Bible does not, it would be a good idea to pray to him before reading it. In the first place, the Spirit gives birth to our desire to open the Bible and read it. Then as we read or listen to Scripture, the Spirit sheds light on the meaning of the text. Father Raniero Cantalamessa, O.F.M. Cap., claims, "The Holy Spirit enkindling light in our minds comes to us when we are reading Scripture more frequently by far than in any other circumstance." Through Scripture, God speaks to us personally. Besides helping us to interpret the Bible, the Holy Spirit illumines our hearts to realize how we can apply the holy words to our lives.

Understanding Scripture passages might not be instantaneous. We need to complement our reading by listening to homilies and talks on the

Bible, consulting biblical commentaries, and joining Bible study groups. Of course, we must also spend time pondering God's Word.

Once we are familiar with Scripture—even memorizing verses—the Holy Spirit reminds us of certain passages at appropriate times.

It is not those passages I do not understand that bother me, but those that I do understand.

~ Mark Twain

Guiding the Church's Interpretation

Fourth, the Holy Spirit watches over the Church constantly, guarding it from error. It follows then that this Spirit of truth is with the Church as she teaches the Scriptures. He also makes the Church the ultimate interpreter of the Word of God. Scripture scholars delve into the meaning of passages by considering such things as the author, audience, purpose, literary style, and the culture at the time they were written. Their insights and theories contribute to our understanding of the Bible. The Church, however, has the last word about God's Word.

Making Us Holy through Scripture

Fifth, Scripture forms us in the spiritual life. In particular, as we engage in the struggle with evil rampant in the world, we might keep in mind a metaphor of St. Paul. He urges us to stand strong by putting on the armor of Christ.

This armor includes "the sword of the Spirit, which is the word of God" (Ephesians 6:17). So arm yourself by meditating on Scripture verses.

Ignorance of Scripture is ignorance of Christ.

~ Saint Jerome

Reflection/Discussion

• When has Scripture struck you like a lightning bolt as you heard or read it?

• How can you integrate the reading of Scripture in your daily life?

• What are your favorite Scripture passages? Why?

Prayer

Holy Spirit, may my heart be open to the Word of God, may my heart be open to good, may my heart be open to the beauty of God, every day. ~ Pope Francis

Action

You hear the Scripture read at Mass, but you might read it at home to connect with God too. Keep a Bible near your bed and each night read a couple verses. Or begin each day by reading a passage or the readings of the Mass of the day, which can be found in booklets or on the Internet.

7

The Holy Spirit and the Eucharist

At the center of the Church is the Eucharist,
where Christ is present and active in humanity
and in the whole world by means of the Holy Spirit.
~ Pope St. John Paul II

Because the Eucharist is the source and summit of Christian life, naturally the Holy Spirit, who is the artisan of our spiritual life, is deeply involved in it. In fact, the effectiveness of all the sacraments is attributed to the Holy Spirit.

In the Eucharistic liturgy, Christ's saving acts—his passion, death, and resurrection—are made present today, reenacted. You are able to participate in the mystery of salvation over and over. The Holy Spirit, who facilitated the original Paschal Mystery in Jerusalem, makes this possible. Throughout the Mass, the Spirit is active in the events occurring at the altar, in your heart, and in the people worshiping with you.

First of all, the Spirit prompts you to go to Mass when you might prefer to stay in bed, go golfing, or finish some work. He gathers you and the other children of God together for the great act of worship in which we have a foretaste of the union we will have with God in heaven.

Opening Rites

Early Christian tabernacles were often in the form of a dove, a symbol of the Holy Spirit.

Mass begins with the Sign of the Cross in which the Three Persons are named. Then during the penitential rite the Spirit inspires you to realize your sins and feel remorse. This rite may be replaced by the blessing and sprinkling of holy water, a reminder of your baptism. In this case, the celebrant begins by inviting us to ask God to keep us faithful to the Holy Spirit we received.

Next the Spirit prays in you as you praise God in the "Gloria." At the end of this prayer, you proclaim that Jesus is the Most High with the Holy Spirit, in the glory of God the Father.

The Liturgy of the Word

As the reading(s) and Gospel are proclaimed and the psalm is read or sung, the Spirit recalls for you the meaning of the Paschal Mystery celebrated at the sacrament. He opens your ears and heart to hear and respond to God's Word.

Then the Spirit helps you to focus on the homily instead of daydreaming or planning the next meal. He has also inspired the homilist to break open Scripture in a meaningful way.

Following that, the Holy Spirit stirs your faith so you profess the Creed wholeheartedly and then join in offering the universal prayers.

The Offering

The Holy Spirit, whom you received as gift, supports your prayers as you offer to God yourself as gift—all that you have and all your works. He also enables you to offer the bread and wine that will become a sacrifice to benefit the entire human race.

The Heart of the Mass

When Mary, a virgin, asked how she would become the mother of the Son of the Most High, the Angel Gabriel replied, "The Holy Spirit will come upon you, and the power of the Most High will overshadow you" (Luke 1:35). In view of this miracle, there is no need to ask with skepticism, "How can bread become Christ and wine his blood?" Nevertheless, St. John of Damascus answers, "The power of the Holy Spirit will be at work to give us a marvel which surpasses understanding."

The *Catechism of the Catholic Church* says, "At the heart of the Eucharistic celebration are the bread and wine that, by the words of Christ and the invocation of the Holy Spirit, become Christ's Body and Blood." (#1333) The fourth century Church Father St. John Chrysostom expressed this miraculous change poetically, perhaps in a Christmas homily:

Our Eucharistic banquet: "Enrich your soul in the great goodness of God: The Father is your table, the Son is your food, and the Holy Spirit waits on you and then makes his dwelling in you.

~ Saint Catherine of Siena

According to tradition, the month of April is dedicated to the Holy Spirit and the Blessed Sacrament.

If we approach with faith, we too will see Jesus . . . for the Eucharistic table takes the place of the crib. Here the Body of the Lord is present, wrapped not in swaddling clothes but in the rays of the Holy Spirit.

The part of the Mass in which the celebrant calls for the help of the Holy Spirit is known as the epiclesis, from the Greek for "invocation" or "summon." In this prayer we ask that the Holy Spirit make our gifts of bread and wine holy and transform them into the Body and Blood of Christ.

Believing that bread and wine become Jesus Christ is a miracle in itself. Maybe on occasion you have doubts about it. The Holy Spirit can infuse you with the robust faith needed to accept what seems impossible.

Besides asking the Holy Spirit to change the bread and wine into Christ, we pray at Mass that those who partake of the Body and Blood of Jesus may become one body by the Holy Spirit. The Spirit who unites the Father and Son is the great unifier who can make us grow in unity, making us one in mind and heart.

The Eucharistic prayer concludes with a prayer of praise to the Trinity. The presider prays that all honor and glory be to the Father; through, with, and in the Son; and in the unity of the Holy Spirit. With the help of the Spirit, you respond with a resounding "Amen!"

—

Dew as Symbol

In Eucharistic Prayer II, we pray that the gifts are made holy by the Spirit coming upon them "like dewfall." That comparison might strike you as odd, but dew is an apt symbol for the Holy Spirit. Dew forms when water vapor condenses and appears silently during the night. It covers the ground and nurtures the growth of grass and plants. In the desert the Israelites were fed each morning when dew evaporated and revealed manna. At Mass we rely on the Spirit to provide sacred bread. You can ask the Holy Spirit to soak you that you might become bread for others.

Communion and Dismissal

The Communion rite opens with an Our Father. The Spirit who enables us to call God "Father" helps you pray this prayer with devotion.

Because the Persons of the Trinity are one, when you receive Jesus in Communion, you also receive the Father and the Holy Spirit. During this time the Spirit assists you in making a good thanksgiving after Communion: adoring, loving, thanking, and asking forgiveness of your Lord and Savior.

In Communion not only are you united with Christ, but with all the members of his body, the Church—everyone in the communion of saints: on Earth, in purgatory, and in heaven.

At the center of the Church is the Eucharist, where Christ is present and active in humanity and in the world by means of the Holy Spirit.

~ Saint Pope John Paul II

St. Ignatius of Antioch called the Eucharist the medicine of immortality and the antidote against death.

Finally, nourished by the Eucharist and fortified by the Holy Spirit, you are empowered to go forth, live the Gospel, and spread the Good News. You are not alone. The Holy Spirit goes every step of the way with you.

Reflection/Discussion

• Why do you believe that at Mass bread and wine become the body and blood of Jesus?

• How can you become more aware and more appreciative of the great mystery that takes place at every Eucharistic celebration?

• What was the most memorable Mass you ever attended? Why?

Prayer

O Holy Spirit, sweet Guest of my soul, abide in me,
and grant that I may ever abide in thee. Amen.

Action

At the next Eucharist you participate in, listen for references to the Holy Spirit. Thank him for making the death and resurrection of Jesus and the Eucharist possible.

8

The Holy Spirit and You

As the sunbeam illumines a transparent substance,
making it brilliant, so too, Spirit-bearing souls,
illumined by him, become spiritual themselves,
sending their grace forth to others.
~ St. Basil

Before taking a test, Catholic children used to pray: "Holy Spirit, Lord of Light, help me choose the one that's right." The Holy Spirit can do more for you than help you pass tests. The source of your relationship with God, he has been at work in you and at your service ever since your baptism.

The date of your baptism is as significant as the date of your birth. Likewise, it is a time for celebration and gratitude to God. Jesus taught, "No one can enter the kingdom of God without being born of water and Spirit" (John 3:3, 5). Yes, your baptism was your key to heaven. Through it you were reborn and sanctified by receiving supernatural life, divine life, which is also called sanctifying grace. The Trinity came to dwell in you, and God began to live through you. You shared in the nature of God and became godlike. And you participated in eternal love.

God's love has been poured into our hearts through the Holy Spirit that has been given to us.

~ Romans 5:5

In this initial sacrament you were united with Jesus in his death and resurrection, symbolized most vividly in baptism by immersion. Going down into water and coming up again had been the custom in the early Church.

In baptism you became a child of God: "The Spirit Himself bears witness with our spirit that we are children of God, and if children, heirs also, heirs of God and fellow heirs with Christ" (Romans 8:16–17). Your inheritance is nothing less than eternal life in heaven.

Your Personal Pentecost

Your baptism of the Spirit occurred on the day you were baptized. You were possessed by the Holy Spirit. This Third Person dwells in your innermost being, whether you feel his presence or not: "Do you not know that your body is a temple of the Holy Spirit?" (1 Corinthians 6:19). Your baptism was your personal Pentecost. Your life in the Spirit initiated at that time came to maturity at your confirmation.

When Jesus was baptized in the Jordan River, the Father proclaimed, "This is my beloved Son," and the Spirit came down upon him as a dove. This rite prepared him for his mission. So too at your baptism the Spirit came upon you. You were consecrated, set apart, and sealed as a Christian, a follower of Jesus Christ.

You became a member of his Mystical Body, the Church, and someone who is responsible for spreading the Gospel.

Corrie Ten Boom, who hid Jews during the Holocaust, said, "Trying to do the Lord's work in your own strength is the most confusing, exhausting and tedious of all work. But when you are filled with the Holy Spirit, then the ministry of Jesus just flows out of you."

The three sacraments of initiation (Baptism, Confirmation, Eucharist) had been one ceremony with a bishop presiding. Confirmation split from Baptism when there were too many baptisms for bishops to attend. In 1439, the Council of Florence declared it a separate sacrament. Eastern churches still initiate with all three sacraments, usually with a priest presiding.

The Sanctifier

On Pentecost, nine days after Jesus ascended to heaven, the apostles were filled with the Holy Spirit. Their fear gave way to courage, and they burst forth to eagerly proclaim the Good News. That same Spirit began empowering you at your baptism. He serves you in all the ways Jesus promised. But the Spirit doesn't force. You must be open to him. As someone put it, you must catch the wind of God in your sails. Then you must choose to allow him to act. St. Paul advised, "If we live by the Spirit, let us also be guided by the Spirit" (Galatians 5:25).

This is not only to your benefit. Like an artist, the creative Spirit is designing the history of humankind. By surrendering to him and heeding his sometimes mysterious promptings, you add your touches. The finished panorama will be revealed at the end of time.

The Holy Spirit is always with you.

The saints are the master-pieces of the Holy Spirit.

~ Saint Pope John XXIII

The Holy Spirit abides in you forever (unless serious sin drives him out). I learned this during my first year of teaching religion in high school. The students in my class were very bright. Every day they would challenge me and ruin my carefully prepared lesson, in particular a girl named Barbara. Discouraged, I confided to the teacher across the hall that I felt like a failure. She assured me that the Holy Spirit was my partner in the classroom. He was working though me and accomplishing things I might never know. So day after day I went on teaching in sheer faith. Toward the end of the school year, as I corrected tests, I found that Barbara had appended a note to hers. It read, "Sister, you probably won't believe this, but I go to daily Mass and Communion. Something you said a while ago made me realize how important my faith is."

The Holy Spirit sanctifies you.

Father of the poor is a title of the Holy Spirit. You may not be poor materially, but you were poor in that you were once deprived of eternal life. Moreover, as a human, you make wrong decisions and can be prone to egotism, pride, and selfishness. You may have poor motives,

poor thoughts, and poor actions and be subject to unruly passions. The Holy Spirit, however, helps you to be holy.

Scripture guarantees, "All who are led by the Spirit of God are children of God" (Romans 8:14). Paul prayed that Christians may be strengthened in their "inner being with power through his Spirit" (Ephesians 3:16). The Holy Spirit is waiting to be your ally in rooting out your predominant fault. If your spiritual life is frozen, the Holy Spirit can renew it—just like a warm wind melts ice and heralds spring.

The Spirit guides you in following God's laws of love. With the Spirit you can live full of love, even toward those you do not like and outright enemies. According to Silouan the Athonite, "The Holy Spirit teaches us to love our enemies in such a way that we pity their souls as if they were our own children." This may require forgiving those who have harmed you, another difficult thing the Holy Spirit enables you to do.

The Holy Spirit prompts you to do good: to visit the widow down the street, to compliment that obnoxious person, to volunteer for a task when no one else does. The Spirit also empowers you to fight temptation; and when you fail, he piques your conscience to realize your sin. He moves you to remorse and repentance and urges you to seek forgiveness from God. The evangelist Billy Graham said, "For me, the

Someday after we have mastered the winds, the waves, the tides and gravity, we shall harness for God energies of love. Then for the second time in the history of the world, we will have discovered fire.

~ Teilhard de Chardin,

In the *Odes of Solomon,* an early Christian collection, one poem begins, "As the hand moves over the harp and the strings speak, / So sounds in my inward being the Spirit of the Lord, and I speak by His love."

best time to pray is the very moment a tense situation or an unspiritual attitude overtakes me. God the Holy Spirit is always there, ready to help me gain victory in the spiritual battles I face—big or small."

Gradually the Holy Spirit is transforming you into the likeness of Christ. (2 Corinthians 3:18) However, you must cooperate with the movements of the Holy Spirit so his efforts to save you are not in vain. St. Paul warned, "Do not grieve the Holy Spirit of God, with which you were marked with a seal for the day of redemption" (Ephesians 4:30).

In a nutshell, it is the Spirit who provides you with the life-energy to follow Jesus the Way and who guides you on your pilgrimage to heaven.

The Holy Spirit helps you to pray.

St. Ephrem, who lived in the fourth century, wrote hundreds of hymns and poems, introducing music into Christianity. This won him the name "Lyre of the Holy Spirit." Besides inspiring St. Ephrem's sung prayers, the Holy Spirit directed the Church in formulating our traditional prayers, such as the Hail Mary, the Creed, and our liturgies. He also oversaw the development of prayer forms, such as the Rosary, meditation, and centering prayer.

On the personal level, the Holy Spirit gives you the impulse to pray as a daily habit and sometimes spontaneously. He may do this even when you feel you don't have time to pray or on days you find prayer dry and uninspiring. In addition, the Holy Spirit slips ideas into your mind about intentions and people who need your prayers.

The Spirit also prays in you and for you. Scripture affirms this:

Prayer is not what is done by us, but rather what is done by the Holy Spirit in us.

~ Henri Nouwen

> The Spirit helps us in our weakness; for we do not know how to pray as we ought, but that very Spirit intercedes with sighs too deep for words. And God, who searches the heart, knows what is the mind of the Spirit, because the Spirit intercedes for the saints according to the will of God. (Acts 8:26–27).

The consolations you receive in prayer can also be attributed to the Spirit. St. John Vianney said, "You who are not great saints, you still have many moments when you taste the sweetness of prayer and of the presence of God: these are visits of the Holy Spirit." Be grateful for such visitations.

Before praying, especially when you find it difficult to pray, seek the Holy Spirit's assistance. He is a reliable prayer partner and can fire up your spiritual life.

The Holy Spirit comforts you.

Someone I know likes to fall asleep by repeating, "Holy Spirit, comfort me."

Whenever you are in trouble, stressed, or depressed, the Holy Spirit buoys up your spirits and gives you peace and hope. He renews your strength. In the midst of storms, he may remind you that God loves you and is with you. This may be an inner voice or a thought that conveys a comforting message. Or the Spirit will speak comforting words to you through Scripture. The Spirit might send someone to help or cheer you. Perhaps he will act in a surprising way as the following example illustrates.

A friend of mine greatly dreaded her mother's death. But the moment her mother died, surprisingly the woman was calm and at peace. She believes the Holy Spirit was the reason.

A woman who sorely missed her deceased parents wondered if the notion of an afterlife were just wishful thinking. One day she asked them to let her find two pennies as a sign that they still existed. That morning as she cleaned the couch, she found two pennies and a quarter between the cushions. She reasoned that she had asked for two pennies, not 27¢. Later she went to the store. At the checkout counter her bill came to $10.02. She fished in her purse for 2¢ in vain. The man behind her handed her 2¢. She thought, "That doesn't count because I didn't actually find the money. And it was just a coincidence." At home as she tossed her coat off, two pennies fell out of the pocket. She could almost hear her mother saying, "You should have believed in the first place when I sent you 2¢ and threw in the extra quarter."

The Holy Spirit counsels you.

Hallmark romance movies usually center around a character who must decide whether to follow a career or commit to a loved one. At times you too are faced with a major decision such as whom to marry, where to live, what job to take, and whether to have surgery. Or you may be struggling with a sticky moral decision, for example, should I lie to please my boss and keep my job? Perhaps you must confront someone and don't know what to say. Sometimes you are in a situation where you can't decide if you should speak up or keep still.

In these and similar cases, pray to the Holy Spirit for light to know how to proceed. During your life's journey he acts as a spiritual GPS. You only need to be attuned to his directions.

If we live by the Spirit, let us also be guided by the Spirit.

~ Galatians 5:25

The Holy Spirit emboldens you.

Any number of things can terrify you. You may be afraid of flying in a plane or speaking before a group (the number one human fear!). You might be apprehensive about an upcoming job interview, an important meeting, or an intervention. You may dread making a difficult phone call or confronting a person who needs to be confronted. Or you may be asked to undertake a task for which you feel unqualified.

———

When facing situations like these, call on the Holy Spirit for courage. You can simply say, "Holy Spirit, help!" Doing this will give you confidence and keep you calm. Then like St. Paul you can boast, "I can do all things through him who strengthens me" (Philippians 4:13).

For two thousand years Christian martyrs have gone to their death bravely from the first one, the deacon St. Stephen, to the person executed yesterday for believing in Jesus. How did they do it? They were sustained by the Holy Spirit. Third-century theologian Tertullian said that the Holy Spirit was the coach of martyrs. You too can depend on him to help you boldly witness to your faith and defend it in private or in public.

The Holy Spirit enlightens you.

When you struggle with a church teaching or a Scripture passage, the Holy Spirit helps you to understand it. St. Paul knew this: "We have received ... the Spirit that is from God, so that we may understand the gifts bestowed on us by God. And we speak of these things in words not taught by human wisdom but taught by the Spirit" (1 Corinthians 2:12–13).

It could be that you are asked a question about the faith. The Holy Spirit will enable you to answer it or know where to find the answer.

As a boy, St. Vincent Pallotti struggled in school. His mother suggested that he make a novena to the Holy Spirit. Vincent did and afterward, to his teachers' amazement, his intelligence was greatly improved.

The Holy Spirit inspires you with good ideas.

At times a good thought may flash across your mind seemingly from nowhere. It might occur to you to call a sick friend, to volunteer at a food bank, or to go to confession. Chances are insights like these are the Holy Spirit nudging you toward holiness. He then provides the actual grace for you to follow through on his inspirations. Don't be surprised at the results when you are attuned to the Holy Spirit. He is the God of surprises.

Let yourselves be led by the Holy Spirit and, please, do not cage the Holy Spirit.

~ Pope Francis

Light as Symbol

Light is transparent and pure. In Genesis, it was the first thing that God created. Light benefits us by dispelling darkness and enabling us to see. Sunshine not only makes plants and trees grow, but it is healthy for us. It stimulates the production of Vitamin D, which our bodies need. Light also causes joy because it increases seratonin. The Holy Spirit functions like light when he reveals truths to us, makes us realize our sins, and guides us on right paths. He fosters our spiritual life, which leads to happiness.

Keep your soul at peace in order to be able to be attentive and very faithful to the inner movement of the Holy Spirit.

~ Saint Peter Julian Eymard

Did you ever unexpectedly find information you needed in a book, come upon it on the Internet, or hear it from someone? You may consider such an experience a coincidence. Rather, attribute it to the Holy Spirit working for you. Someone defined coincidence as "God acting anonymously."

On Facebook I once requested suggestions for a title for a book I wrote about Mary in which she speaks to the reader every day of the year. None of the replies were satisfactory. One night the title "Heart to Heart with Mary" floated into my mind, but I wasn't sure I liked it. The next morning my cousin, who had seen my post, called and said, "What about "Heart to Heart with Mary"? The idea had come to her the evening before! I must credit the Holy Spirit as the co-author. As I reread that book each day, the writing, which was finished in record time, is unfamiliar and does not seem like mine. It is too good.

Another time as I was selling my books, a young boy wanted a certain one, but he had no money. I am a Slovenian, and we are known for being, shall I say "thrifty"? Moreover, I have taken a vow of poverty and watch my pennies. Nevertheless, the Spirit urged me to give the boy the book for free, and so I did. Afterward his teacher came to me and said, "That boy's mother is battling cancer, and your gift brought a little joy into his life."

Your Response

Most Reverend Luis M. Martinez describes our ideal response to the Holy Spirit in a beautiful, poetic way in his book *The Sanctifier:*

To love this divine Spirit is
to let ourselves be taken along by Him,
as the feather is carried along by the wind;
to let ourselves be possessed by Him,
as the dry branch is possessed by the fire that burns it;
to let ourselves be animated by Him,
as the sensitive strings of a lyre take life
from the artist's touch.

Discernment of Spirits

There is a joke about an obese sister whose superior suggests that she refrain from eating so much. The superior says, "Remember, you are a temple of God and must respect your body." Sometime later, the sister is still overloading her plate with food. Puzzled, the superior comments, "I thought you were going to lose weight." The sister replies, "I was, but then I heard an inner voice say, 'You are not to be a temple but a basilica.'"

So, how do you know if your ideas arise from the Holy Spirit, the evil spirit, or your own

> We have the right, the duty, and the joy to say that Pentecost goes on.
>
> ~ Saint Pope John Paul II

A person's character is the sum total of numerous little choices.

selfishness? There are several touchstones. True inspirations are compatible with Scripture and church teachings, not to mention the Ten Commandments. People who really know you and who are wise and trustworthy can also provide insights concerning the source of your thoughts and assist you in making up your mind as to a course of action. Then too a spiritual director is a valuable asset when it comes to recognizing the true value of your ideas. Last but not least, prayer aids discernment.

Life in the Spirit

On the Jewish Pentecost, the first fruits of the wheat harvest were brought to the temple and offered to God, a sign of more to come. The Christian Pentecost promised similar fruit.

St. Augustine wrote, "If you want to live in the Holy Spirit, preserve charity, love truth, wish for unity, and you will be united with eternity."

How can you tell whether you are living a Spirit-powered life? If you are, you will experience certain perfections known as the twelve fruits of the Holy Spirit. In keeping with this fruit analogy, the Spirit would be a seed. The fruits are the harvest of a morally good life, the result of cooperating with grace. The first six fruits are listed in Galatians 5:22; the last three are from the Vulgate translation of the Bible. By possessing these fruits, you will be more like Jesus. Your life will be a foretaste of the glory you will enjoy in the next world. Notice that each fruit is an aspect of love.

Fruits of the Holy Spirit

Love	Faithfulness
Joy	Gentleness
Peace	Self-control
Patience	Modesty
Kindness	Goodness
Generosity	Chastity

St. Paul often referred to the Christian pilgrimage to heaven as "walking according to the Spirit." This means following God's will and avoiding sin—in other words, living a life of love. One strategy for doing this is to keep focused not on sinful things but on the Spirit and his fruits. Thoughts become actions and actions become habits, which lead to your eternal destiny.

Jesus told a parable about a barren fig tree that would be cut down if after one more year it bore no fruit. (Luke 13:6–9)

Reflection/Discussion

• When have you done something that could only be attributed to supernatural help?

• How can you be more familiar with and at home with the Spirit like the first Christians?

• To what extent does each fruit of the Spirit characterize your life?

Prayer

Breathe in me, O Holy Spirit,
that my thoughts may all be holy.
Act in me, O Holy Spirit,
that my work, too, may be holy.
Draw my heart, O Holy Spirit,
that I love but what is holy.
Strengthen me, O Holy Spirit,
to defend all that is holy.
Guard me, then, O Holy Spirit,
that I always may be holy. Amen.

~ St. Augustine

Action

If you don't know the day of your baptism, find out what it is. Celebrate that day in some way, maybe by going to Mass or spending extra time in prayer.

9

Gifts of the Holy Spirit

By its nature love is enduring. ...We catch a further glimpse of how much the Holy Spirit offers our world: love which dispels uncertainty; love which overcomes the fear of betrayal; love which carries eternity within; the true love which draws us into a unity that abides!

~ Pope Benedict XVI

The greatest gift God has given you is the Holy Spirit. Isn't it astounding that God gives himself to you? You possess God! The intimacy you enjoy with God cannot be surpassed. And the Holy Spirit truly is the gift that keeps on giving—all through your life. He never abandons you but is always actively present. St. Irenaeus dubbed the Holy Spirit "the ladder of our ascent to God." Through the Holy Spirit you come to know and experience Jesus. And through Jesus you are able to know the Father.

St. Peter Damian expressed how necessary the Holy Spirit is: "As the soul is the life of the body, so the Holy Spirit is the life of our souls."

Pope Benedict XVI wrote encyclicals on the theological virtues: *Deus caritas est* (God Is Love), *Spe salvi* (Hope of Salvation), and the draft of *Lumen fidei* (Light of Faith), which Pope Francis finalized.

When the Holy Spirit first came into your soul at baptism, like any considerate guest he came bearing gifts. In fact, he lavishly bestowed on you supernatural gifts far better than precious jewels. For they set you on the track to be holy and fulfill God's dream of eternal happiness for you.

These gifts are not only for you personally but for the church community. Hunger for them that they may be deepened in you and in the Church as a whole.

Theological Virtues

The instant you were baptized, the Holy Spirit infused you with three theological virtues: faith, hope, and charity. Thus they are the result of God's grace. They are revealed in Scripture (Paul named them in 1 Corinthians 13:13) and defined by St. Thomas Aquinas.

A virtue is a power or a good moral trait. *Theological* means pertaining to God. The *Catechism of the Catholic Church* states that the three theological virtues have God for their "origin, motive, and object" (#1812). They establish a relationship between you and God and help you direct your life toward God. They are supernatural and enable you to perform deeds beyond your natural ability in order that you may someday have eternal life.

Faith

Believing in God and God's revelation and trusting in him.

God has graciously provided three channels for revealing truths: creation, Scripture, and Jesus.

Faith illumines knowledge and makes it easy to accept what is true. We can reason to the existence of God, notably the five proofs of St. Thomas Aquinas. But faith gives us assurance. For our limited minds some truths are beyond understanding. Three Persons in one God? The virgin birth? Bread and wine becoming Jesus? Through the grace of the Holy Spirit, we accept doctrines that seem impossible. We take them "on faith."

Hope

Steadfastly looking forward to eternal life confident that God will fulfill his promises.

Hope makes us desire being with God in heaven and strengthens the belief that our insatiable yearning for happiness will be fulfilled someday. It helps us to trust that God will

St. Hilary of Poitiers called the Holy Spirit "the One Gift who bestows perfect hope."

provide the graces necessary to reach heaven. When we are faced with trials and tragedies, hope sustains us and keeps us from becoming discouraged or despairing.

Charity

Love for God and everyone and for everything God created.

We should love God because He is God, and the measure of our love should be to love Him without measure.

~ Saint Bernard

Charity enables us to love God above all things. St. Paul said that this virtue is the most excellent of the three virtues. It outlasts the other two and is the basis of all other virtues. Jesus said the greatest commandment is to love God "with all your heart, and with all our soul, and with all your mind" and the second greatest is to "love your neighbor as yourself." At the Last Supper he also posed the high standard that we are to love others as he has loved us.

+ + +

Praying for these virtues and practicing them will strengthen them. Acts of faith, hope, and love can be found on the website of the United States Conference of Catholic Bishops under "Prayers and Devotions."

Cardinal Moral Virtues

Stemming from the theological virtues are the cardinal moral virtues that enable you to make right judgments and act like a Christian. These moral virtues are not infused by the Holy Spirit but developed by learning about them and practicing them until they become habits. They are called "cardinal" from the Latin for "hinge" because all virtues depend on them.

Prudence

Seeing things clearly, knowing what is right and what is wrong, and choosing what is good. It guides our judgment and conscience.

Justice

Giving God and neighbor what is rightfully theirs and respecting the rights of others. The Second Vatican Council called for a renewed focus on social justice.

Fortitude

Facing trials, difficulties, and danger bravely and persevering in doing good. This virtue also helps us deal with temptations and witness to Christ in the face of obstacles.

Temperance

Enjoying pleasures and the things of this world in moderation. It is the self-control that restrains our appetites and passions.

Seven Gifts of the Holy Spirit

Six of the gifts are named in Isaiah 11:1–2 as being found in the Messiah upon whom the spirit rests.

In addition, the Spirit showered seven other supernatural gifts on you at baptism. He then strengthened them at your confirmation when the bishop anointed you with chrism and said, "Be sealed with the gift of the Holy Spirit." Seven signifies perfection and completion. The seven gifts strengthen your faith, make your hope more constant, and intensify your charity.

These gifts are dispositions to follow the Holy Spirit's promptings easily, instinctively. They enable you to live a good life in ways that are beyond merely human effort. You might pray for a deepening of one or all of these gifts.

Wisdom

Wisdom is knowing and loving God, resulting in a great longing to be with him. Pope Francis defined this gift as "seeing with God's eyes, listening with God's ears, loving with God's heart, judging things with God's judgment." With wisdom you have deep insight into the truths of our faith, value them, and live by them. You also have a right relationship with God's creation, seeing all things as gifts from God. Wisdom is the greatest of the seven gifts.

St. Thérèse of Lisieux took no theology courses, but her wisdom garnered her the title Doctor of the Church.

Understanding

Understanding is grasping the meaning of the revealed truths of our faith easily and deeply perhaps with a flash of insight. When you understand these truths better, your faith is bolstered. With this gift you also know what is important in life and value the right things.

By virtue of the seven gifts of the Holy Spirit, all evils are destroyed and all good things are produced.

~ Saint Bonaventure

The great theologian St. Thomas Aquinas had such an understanding of the faith that he produced volumes like the classic *Summa Theologica*, a collection of all the teachings of the Church and the reasoning behind them. Yet after a mystical experience, he refused to write, saying, "All that I've written seems like straw to me."

Counsel

Counsel is making moral judgments that maintain a good relationship with God and others. It intuitively lets you know the course of action to choose that will please and glorify God. In other words, it helps you know good from evil. This gift also gives you insights to advise other people.

St. Francis de Sales was a renowned spiritual director who counseled numerous people. His influence continues today through his book *Introduction to the Devout Life,* in which he offers practical ways to attain holiness.

Fortitude

Fortitude is firmly withstanding difficulties and dangers that are encountered because of being a follower of Christ. With fortitude you have strength to witness to the faith and perhaps suffer for it. This gift also enables you to accept crosses, bear trials, and undertake challenging tasks courageously and perhaps for a long time.

For refusing to acknowledge King Henry VIII as head of the Church in England, St. Thomas More was imprisoned. Despite pressure to submit and save his life, he bravely held firm and was beheaded.

Knowledge

Knowledge is seeing ourselves, others, and situations from God's perspective and in harmony with our faith. Knowledge leads you to act as God wishes and helps you to see the divine purpose in whatever happens. With knowledge you can discern temptations and inspirations.

St. Joan of Arc knew she had to lead the French army in driving out the English in the Hundred Years' War and see that Charles VII was made king. A soldier reported that Joan said, "I would rather have remained spinning at my mother's side . . . yet must I go and must I do this thing, for my Lord wills that I do so."

The Spirit of God is always pressing our souls to fulfill His mysterious purpose for each one of us, and our peace consists in obedience to the pressure.

~ Evelyn Underhill

Piety

Piety is revering and trusting God as a loving Father and respecting all he has created. Piety impels you to pray and to give God glory. With it you love and obey God as you would a parent. You do what is good and right out of love for God, not out of fear. Piety also enables you to respect and obey lawful authorities.

Juliana of Norwich wrote, "Just as God is our Father, so God is also our Mother." She advised that we thank and praise God for having created us, pray to our Mother to obtain mercy, and pray to the Holy Spirit for help and grace. Her devotion to this God, who loved us even before he created us, compelled her to become an anchoress. She devoted her entire life to prayer and good works, living in seclusion in a room next to the church of St. Julian.

St. Juliana wrote *Revelations of Divine Love,* the earliest extant book in English written by a woman.

Fear of the Lord

Fear of the Lord is a positive gift, for it does not mean being afraid of God's anger and punishment. Rather, it means being filled with wonder and awe at the majesty of God, the Supreme Being. This gift leads you to have a profound reverence for God. Consequently, it fosters a desire in you to please such a great God. Therefore you avoid offending him by sin. Fear of the Lord is an antidote to temptations.

After one encounter with the risen, glorified Jesus, Saul, a chief persecutor of the Church, became a zealous Christian (Paul). Consumed by a burning desire to glorify God, he founded churches, converted Gentiles, and wrote letters incorporated in the Bible. As Paul spread the Good News, he was subjected to much suffering and persecution and was martyred.

I regard everything as loss because of the surpassing value of knowing Christ Jesus my Lord.

~Philippians 3:8

Charisms

Unlike the virtues, which develop your personal relationship with God, a charism is a special gift that the Holy Spirit bestows for the good of others, the world, and especially the Church. As such, they are ways to serve God and others. The word *charism* is from the Greek for grace or favor. St. Paul lists some of these charisms in 1 Corinthians 12:8–10 as follows:

> Wisdom
> Knowledge
> Faith
> Healing
> Working of miracles
> Prophecy
> Discernment of spirits
> Speaking in tongues
> Interpretation of tongues

Granted, those charisms that are deemed extraordinary today are thought by some to be restricted to the first Christians. However, they are characteristic of the relatively recent charismatic movement. This form of spirituality began for mainline Protestants around 1960. For Catholics, it arose in 1967 at Duquesne University in Pittsburgh and became known as the Catholic Charismatic Renewal. This movement, features a personal encounter with God, referred to as "baptism in the Holy Spirit." (Your baptism with water was essentially baptism in the Holy Spirit.)

People who experience this new influx of the Holy Spirit may begin speaking in tongues as a sign of their "baptism." More important, they are blessed with a renewed commitment to Christ and great peace and joy. Charismatic prayer services involve the lifting of hands, prophecy, speaking in tongues (glossolalia), singing in tongues, interpretation of tongues, healings, and testimonies (reports of what God is doing in one's life).

One phenomenon associated with charismatics is being slain in the Spirit or resting in the Spirit. A person overcome by the Spirit falls gently to the ground and remains there, resting in peace and joy. Some people understand this as a manifestation of the Holy Spirit, while others attribute it to an individual's emotional response, hypnosis, or the devil.

[The Holy Spirit] comes to the ones who love him, who invite him, who eagerly await him.

~ Saint Bonaventure

Those who are unspiritual do not receive the gifts of God's Spirit, for they are foolishness to them, and they are unable to understand them.

~ 1 Corinthians 2:14

The Holy Spirit truly transforms us. With our cooperation, he also wants to transform the world we live in.

~ Pope Francis

The Church declares about all these gifts: "Whether these charisms be very remarkable or more simple and widely diffused, they are to be received with thanksgiving and consolation since they are fitting and useful for the needs of the Church." (*Dogmatic Constitution on the Church*, #12) You might pray to be blessed with one of these charisms.

Cardinal Mercier of Belgium explained the purpose of your supernatural gifts:

Through an ever closer adherence to the Holy Spirit in the sanctuary of your soul, you can, from within your home circle, in the heart of your country, within the limits of your parish, pass over all earthly frontiers, and by your work, your purity of life, your participation in the common lot of suffering, intensify and extend the Kingdom of Love.

Reflection/Discussion

• St. Paul identifies love as greater than faith and hope. Why would he say this?

• Which of the seven gifts is the strongest in your life?

• Which gift would you like to cultivate more?

Prayer

O Lord Jesus Christ, before ascending into heaven
you did promise to send the Holy Spirit to finish your work
in the souls of your Apostles and Disciples.
deign to grant the same Holy Spirit to me
that he may perfect in my soul
the work of your grace and your love.

Grant me the Spirit of Wisdom
   that I may despise the perishable things of this world
   and aspire only after the things that are eternal,
the Spirit of Understanding
   to enlighten my mind with the light of your divine truth,
the Spirit of Counsel that may ever choose the surest way
   of pleasing God and gaining heaven,
the Spirit of Fortitude
   that I may bear my cross with you
   and that I may overcome with courage
   all the obstacles that oppose my salvation,
the Spirit of Knowledge
   that I may know God and know myself
   and grow perfect in imitation of the Saints,
the Spirit of Piety
   that I may find the service of God sweet and amiable,
and the Spirit of Fear
   that I may be filled with a loving reverence toward God
   and may dread in any way to displease him.

Mark me, dear Lord, with the sign of your true disciples
and animate me in all things with your Spirit. Amen.

Action

Go out of your way today to perform a loving act for some-one, preferably someone for whom you have a natural aversion or someone who hurt you. You might do a favor, offer to help, write a kind note, or pray for the person.

10

Delighting in the Holy Spirit

Spirit of the Living God, fall afresh on me.
Melt me, mold me, fill me, use me.
~ Daniel Iverson

One Sunday as I was playing the piano for the residents of the retirement village where I live, a widow with her oxygen tank in tow came in from outside. She walked up to me and asked, "Were you just playing 'Ah, Sweet Mystery of Life'?" "Yes," I replied. "Would you please play that song again. It was my wedding song." She stood beside the piano while I complied. When I finished repeating the song, the woman said with tears in her eyes, "Today is my husband's birthday."

Note the many coincidences in this happening. Sometimes you have to believe that Someone is behind the scenes in life, orchestrating them. And that Someone is the Holy Spirit. Beyond the initial act of creating the universe, the Spirit orders its events. Often he surprises us in ways that overwhelm us, bringing great delight.

When you are aware of the constant presence of the Spirit, you can sense him working not only in the world at large but in your heart.

Your Companion

A friend has been defined as someone who knows all about you and likes you anyway.

The Holy Spirit is your intimate friend. What a source of joy his companionship can be for you! At all times the Spirit—this all-powerful God who has crazy love for you—lives in the depths of your being. You are never alone. That is a comforting thought, especially when you face a challenge, hardship, or danger. Knowing that the Holy Spirit is always acting for you, brings about a deep-down calm and peace in the midst of any storm.

After I give a talk, usually I realize that I inadvertently omitted certain ideas or stories. This bothered me until someone pointed out that the Spirit guided my presentation and what I did say was what people needed to hear. What I neglected to say either wasn't important or possibly could have led to trouble.

Your Guide to Happiness

You were made for happiness, and therefore you long for it. Nothing promoted by ads, no success or accomplishment, and no person on Earth will leave you completely satisfied. You feel restless because you are homesick. You belong with your Father in heaven, where you will experience total bliss. The only path there is the path of love.

Out of compassion, God sent the Holy Spirit to lead you to your lost home by prompting you to do loving deeds and restraining you from submitting to temptations. He plays a critical role in helping you stand firm against egotism, selfishness, greed, lust, jealousy, and anything else that would make you less worthy of eternal life. He makes you delight in following his inner urges.

My vocation is love.

~ Saint Thérèse of Lisieux

Because of the Holy Spirit, you can live out your days with confidence rather than anxiety. A proper response to him would be Dag Hammarskjöld's words: "For all that has been, Thanks. For all that will be, Yes."

A story from the desert fathers teaches a profound lesson:

> Abba Lot came to Abba Joseph and said: Father, according as I am able, I keep my little rule, and my little fast, my prayer, meditation and contemplative silence, and I strive to cleanse my heart of evil thoughts. What more should I do? The elder rose up and stretched out his hands to heaven, and his fingers became like ten lamps of fire. He said: "If you will, you can become fire."

With the assistance of the Holy Spirit, you can be on fire with love and enflame others who are in contact with you. In time, you will be holy, a saint!

Reflection/Discussion

As the sun can be seen only by its own light, so Christ can be known only by his own Spirit.

~ Robert Leighton

• When has the Holy Spirit made his presence known to you? Has he come to your rescue?

• How does one "become fire" as Abba Joseph recommended?

• How has your attitude toward the Holy Spirit changed by reading this book? What new insights did you acquire?

Prayer

Wind of Inspiration, Creative Spirit of God
    teach me not to forget
    that you come always as gift.
Remind me always to be ready
    to receive and romance and dance with joy
    wherever and whenever you visit
    or risk that you may move on without me.
May I ever be sensitive to your gentle breezes
    and willing to soar with your wild winds.

               Edward M. Hays

Action

In conversation introduce the Holy Spirit as a topic. Share what you know about him and the crucial role he plays in our faith life.

Appendix

More Prayers to the Holy Spirit

Prayers to the Holy Spirit

Without the Holy Spirit, all is cold.
Therefore, when we feel we are losing our fervor,
we must instantly start a novena to the Holy Spirit
to ask for faith and love.
~ St. John Vianney, the Cure of Ars

The Church honors the Holy Spirit in its liturgy by two solemnities. Pentecost Sunday occurs fifty days after Easter; *pentecost* is from the Greek for "fiftieth." This day commemorates the conclusion of the Paschal Mystery: the coming of the Holy Spirit upon the Church. A week later we celebrate Trinity Sunday in honor of the Father, Son, and Holy Spirit.

A votive Mass of the Holy Spirit can be offered anytime. Catholic schools often open the scholastic year with this Mass. A Red Mass is a Mass celebrated specifically for members of the legal profession. The presider wears red vestments to signify the flames of fire associated with the Holy Spirit. The congregation asks the Holy Spirit to guide those present in seeking justice. In October, prior to the Supreme Court's new term, a Red Mass is celebrated at the Cathedral of St. Matthew the Apostle in Washington, D.C.

Novena to the Holy Spirit

A novena is nine days of prayer. The first one occurred before Pentecost at the Lord's request. His disciples prayed for nine days as they awaited the Holy Spirit. Several novenas to the Holy Spirit are available in booklet form and on the Internet.

O Holy Spirit, O my God, I adore Thee, and acknowledge, here in Thy divine presence, that I am nothing and can do nothing without Thee. Come, great Paraclete, Thou father of the poor, Thou comforter the best, fulfill the promise of our blessed Savior, Who would not leave us orphans, and come into the mind and the heart of Thy poor, unworthy creature, as Thou didst descend on the sacred day of Pentecost on the holy Mother of Jesus and on His first disciples. Grant that I may participate in those gifts which Thou didst communicate to them so wonderfully, and with so much mercy and generosity. Take from my heart whatever is not pleasing to Thee, and make of it a worthy dwelling-place for Thyself. Illumine my mind, that I may see and understand the things that are for my eternal good. Inflame my heart with pure love of Thee, that I may be cleansed from the dross of all inordinate attachments, and that my whole life may be hidden with Jesus in God. Strengthen my will, that I may be made conformable to Thy divine will, and be guided by Thy holy inspirations. Aid me by Thy grace to practice the divine lessons of humility, poverty, obedience, and contempt of the world, which Jesus taught us in His mortal life.

Oh, rend the heavens, and come down, consoling Spirit! that inspired and encouraged by Thee, I may faithfully comply with the duties of my state, carry my daily cross most patiently, and endeavor to accomplish the divine will with the utmost perfection. Spirit of love! Spirit of purity! Spirit of peace! Sanctify my soul more and more, and give me that heavenly peace which the world cannot give. Bless our Holy Father the Pope, bless the Church, bless our bishops, our priests, all Religious Orders, and all the faithful, that they may be filled with the spirit of Christ and labor earnestly for the spread of His kingdom.

O Holy Spirit, Thou Giver of every good and perfect gift, grant me, I beseech Thee, the intentions of this novena. May Thy will be done in me and through me. Mayest Thou be praised and glorified forevermore! Amen.

Chaplet of the Holy Spirit

This chaplet in honor of the Holy Spirit consists of three small beads after the crucifix, five groups of seven beads, and two large beads before each group and at the end. The five groups are in remembrance of the five wounds of Jesus that won the grace the Holy Spirit imparts to us. Here are directions for praying the chaplet:

Beads

First small bead: The Sign of the Cross
Second small bead: An act of contrition
Third small bead: The hymn "Come Holy Ghost"
First large bead: An Our Father
Second large bead: A Hail Mary
Each set of seven beads: Glory Be prayers

Conclusion

The Apostles' Creed
An Our Father, Hail Mary, and Glory Be for the intention of the Holy Father.

Mysteries

During each set of beads, a mystery of the Holy Spirit is pondered:

First mystery
    Jesus is conceived of the Blessed Virgin Mary
    by the Holy Spirit.

Second mystery
    The Spirit of the Lord rested upon Jesus when he
    was baptized.

Third mystery
    The Spirit led Jesus into the desert where he was
    tempted by the devil.

Fourth mystery:
    The Holy Spirit is in the Church.

Fifth mystery
    The Holy Spirit dwells in the souls of just men
    and women.

Act of Consecration to the Holy Spirit

O Holy Spirit,
Divine Spirit of light and love,
I consecrate to you my understanding, heart, and will,
my whole being for time and eternity.
May my understanding be always submissive
to your heavenly inspirations
and to the teaching of the Catholic Church,
of which you are the infallible guide;
may my heart be ever inflamed
with love of God and of my neighbor;
may my will be ever conformed to the divine will;
and may my whole life be a faithful imitation of the life
and virtues of our Lord and Savior Jesus Christ,
to whom with the Father and you, O Holy Spirit,
be honor and glory forever. Amen.

St. Pope Pius X

Litany of the Holy Spirit

Lord, have mercy on us.
Christ, have mercy on us.
Lord, have mercy on us.
Father all powerful, have mercy on us.
Jesus, Eternal Son of the Father, Redeemer of the world,
    save us.
Spirit of the Father and the Son, boundless Life of both,
    sanctify us.

Holy Trinity,
    hear us.
Holy Spirit, Who proceeds from the Father and the Son,
    enter our hearts.
Holy Spirit, Who are equal to the Father and the Son,
    enter our hearts.

Response: Have mercy on us.

Promise of God the Father,
Ray of heavenly light,
Author of all good,
Source of heavenly water,
Consuming Fire,
Ardent Charity,
Spiritual Unction,
Spirit of love and truth,
Spirit of wisdom and understanding,
Spirit of counsel and fortitude,
Spirit of knowledge and piety,
Spirit of the fear of the Lord,
Spirit of grace and prayer,
Spirit of peace and meekness,
Spirit of modesty and innocence,
Holy Spirit, the Comforter,
Holy Spirit, the Sanctifier,
Holy Spirit, Who governs the Church,
Gift of God the Most High,
Spirit Who fills the universe,
Spirit of the adoption of the children of God,
    have mercy on us.

Holy Spirit, inspire us with horror of sin.
Holy Spirit, come and renew the face of the earth.
Holy Spirit, shed your Light into our souls.
Holy Spirit, engrave your law in our hearts.
Holy Spirit, inflame us with the flame of your love.
Holy Spirit, open to us the treasures of your graces.
Holy Spirit, teach us to pray well.
Holy Spirit, enlighten us with your heavenly inspirations.
Holy Spirit, lead us in the way of salvation.
Holy Spirit, grant us the only necessary knowledge.
Holy Spirit, inspire in us the practice of good.
Holy Spirit, grant us the merits of all virtues.
Holy Spirit, make us persevere in justice.
Holy Spirit, be our everlasting reward.

Lamb of God, who takes away the sins of the world,
    send us your Holy Spirit.
Lamb of God, who takes away the sins of the world,
    pour down into our souls the gifts of the Holy Spirit.
Lamb of God, who takes away the sins of the world,
    grant us the Spirit of wisdom and piety.

Come, Holy Spirit! Fill the hearts of your faithful,
    and enkindle in them the fire of your love.

Let us pray.
Grant, O merciful Father, that your Divine Spirit may enlighten, inflame and purify us, that he may penetrate us with his heavenly dew and make us fruitful in good works, through Our Lord Jesus Christ, your Son, who with you, in the unity of the same Spirit, lives and reigns forever and ever. Amen.

Come, Holy Spirit (*Veni, Sancte Spiritus*)

This sequence in honor of the Holy Spirit is prayed at Mass on Pentecost after the second reading and before the Gospel. It dates back to the thirteenth century and is sometimes referred to as the Golden Sequence.

Come, Holy Spirit, come!
And from your celestial home
  Shed a ray of light divine!

Come, Father of the poor!
Come, source of all our store!
  Come, within our bosoms shine!

You, of comforters the best;
You, the soul's most welcome guest;
  Sweet refreshment here below;

In our labor, rest most sweet;
Grateful coolness in the heat;
  Solace in the midst of woe.

O most blessed Light divine,
Shine within these hearts of yours,
  And our inmost being fill!

Where you are not, man has naught,
Nothing good in deed or thought,
  Nothing free from taint of ill.

Heal our wounds, our strength renew;
On our dryness pour your dew;
  Wash the stains of guilt away:

Bend the stubborn heart and will;
Melt the frozen, warm the chill;
  Guide the steps that go astray.

On the faithful, who adore
And confess you, evermore
  In your sev'nfold gift descend;

Give them virtue's sure reward;
Give them your salvation, Lord;
  Give them joys that never end. Amen.
    Alleluia.

Come, Holy Ghost (*Veni, Creator*)

This ninth-century hymn that is set to Gregorian chant is sung at solemn events such as ordinations, the consecration of bishops, councils, and the sacrament of Confirmation.

Come, Holy Ghost, Creator, come
from thy bright heav'nly throne;
come, take possession of our souls,
and make them all thine own.

Thou who art called the Paraclete,
best gift of God above,
the living spring, the living fire,
sweet unction and true love.

Thou who art sevenfold in thy grace,
finger of God's right hand;
his promise, teaching little ones
to speak and understand.

O guide our minds with thy blest light,
with love our hearts inflame;
and with thy strength, which ne'er decays,
confirm our mortal frame.

Far from us drive our deadly foe;
true peace unto us bring;
and through all perils lead us safe
beneath thy sacred wing.

Through thee may we the Father know,
through thee th'eternal Son,
and thee the Spirit of them both,
thrice-blessed three in One.

All glory to the Father be,
with his coequal Son;
the same to thee, great Paraclete,
while endless ages run.

Amen.

Prayer of St. John Vianney

O God, send me Thy Spirit to teach me what I am
and what Thou art.

Byzantine Liturgy, Troparion of the Pentecost Vespers

Heavenly Sovereign, Paraclete, Spirit of truth who are present everywhere and who fill all, treasure chest of every good and giver of life, come, live in us, cleanse us of every stain and, you who are good, save our souls. Amen.

Prayer of St. Therese Couderc

Love of the Holy Spirit, be the origin of all the workings of my soul, so that all may be in harmony with the divine good pleasure! Amen!

Prayer of St. Mary Magdalene de Pazzi

Come, Holy Spirit.

Spirit of truth, you are the reward of the saints, the comforter of souls, light in the darkness, riches to the poor, treasure to lovers, food for the hungry, comfort to those who are wandering; to sum up, you are the one in whom all treasures are contained.

Come! As you descended upon Mary that the Word might become flesh, work in us through grace as you worked in her through nature and grace.

Come! Food of every chaste thought, fountain of all mercy, sum of all purity.

Come! Consume in us whatever prevents us from being consumed in you.

Prayer of St. Hildegard of Bingen

Holy Spirit, the life that gives life:
You are the cause of all movement.
You are the breath of all creatures.
You are the salve that purifies our souls.
You are the ointment that heals our wounds.
You are the fire that warms our hearts.
You are the light that guides our feet.
Let all the world praise you.

Prayer of Adam of St. Victor

Who is this who smothers me with the most fragrant perfume?
Who is this who transforms my ugliness into perfect beauty?
Who is this who gives me the sweetest wine to drink and the
finest food to eat?

It is you, Holy Spirit. You turn me into a bride fit for Jesus
Christ. You give me wine and food fit for a wedding in heaven.
My heart was weary, but now it is eager for love. My soul was
sad, but now it is full of joy.

Jesus gave his life for me. Now you, Holy Spirit, give me to
him.

Prayer of St. Ildefonsus

I pray, I pray, O Holy Virgin, that I receive Jesus by that Spirit
who enabled you to conceive Jesus…. May I love Jesus in that
same Spirit in whom you adore him as your Lord and
contemplate him as your Son.

Native American Prayer

Oh, Great Spirit,
Whose voice I hear in the winds
and whose breath gives life to all the world.
Hear me! I need your strength and wisdom.
Let me walk in beauty and make my eyes
ever hold the red and purple sunset.
Make my hands respect the things you have made
and my ears sharp to hear your voice.

Make me wise so that I may understand
the things you have taught my people.
Let me learn the lessons you have hidden
in every leaf and rock.
Help me remain calm and strong in the
face of all that comes towards me.
Help me find compassion without
empathy overwhelming me.

I seek strength, not to be greater than my brother,
but to fight my greatest enemy: myself.
Make me always ready to come to you
with clean hands and straight eyes.
So when life fades, as the fading sunset,
my spirit may come to you without shame.

Translated by Lakota Sioux Chief Yellow Lark in 1887

+ + +

Other prayers to the Holy Spirit can be found at
https://bit.ly/2tsmbaA.

A Few of Sister Kathleen's Other Books

Heart to Heart with Mary
A Yearly Devotional

Praying on Empty
A Guide to Rediscovering Your Prayerful Self

The Fisherman's Wife:
The Gospel According to St. Peter's Spouse

The Catholic Companion to Mary

I Am Going . . .
Reflections on the Last Words of the Saints

The Walking Love of God:
St. Julie Billiart

Praying with Scripture
The Bible: You've Got Mail

The Catholic Way to Pray
An Essential Guide for Adults

The Catholic Companion to Jesus

The Catholic Companion to the Psalms

The Heartbeat of Faith
59 Poems, Fingerplays, and Prayers

Why Is Jesus in the Microwave?
Funny Stores from Catholic Classrooms

Voices ~ God Speaking in Creation
Reflections

A REQUEST

If you like this book,
The Holy Spirit: Font of Love, Life, and Power,
kindly put a review of it at www.amazon.com.
A sentence or two will do.

This will encourage others to nurture
their relationship with this too often forgotten
Third Person of the Trinity.

Made in the USA
Columbia, SC
01 September 2021